D1636988

BLACKS IN THE AMERICAN WEST

EDITORS
Richard Newman
Marcia Renée Sawyer

The involvement of blacks at every point in the exploration, history, and ongoing life of the American West remains a little-known story. The books—both fiction and nonfiction—in this series aim to preserve these stories and to celebrate the achievement and culture of early African-American westerners.

H. C. BRUCE.

THE NEW MAN

Twenty-nine Years a Slave, Twenty-nine Years a Free Man

Recollections of H. C. Bruce

Introduction to the Bison Books Edition
by Willard B. Gatewood

University of Nebraska Press
Lincoln and London

Introduction © 1996 by the University of Nebraska Press
Manufactured in the United States of America

‾ The paper in this book meets the minimum requirements of American
National Standard for Information Sciences—Permanence of Paper for
Printed Library Materials, ANSI Z39.48-1984.

First Bison Books printing: 1996
Most recent printing indicated by the last digit below:
10   9   8   7   6   5   4   3   2   1

Library of Congress Cataloging-in-Publication Data
Bruce, Henry Clay, 1836–1902.
The new man: twenty-nine years a slave, twenty-nine years a free man:
recollections of H. C. Bruce / introduction to the Bison Books edition by
Willard B. Gatewood.
p.   cm.—(Blacks in the American West)
Originally published: York, Pa.: P. Anstadt, 1895.
Includes bibliographical references.
ISBN 0-8032-6132-2 (alk. paper)
1. Bruce, Henry Clay, 1836–1902.   2. Slaves—United States—Biography.
3. Freedmen—United States—Biography.   4. Slavery—Missouri.
5. Missouri—History—Civil War, 1861–1865.   6. Kansas—History—Civil
War, 1861–1865.   7. Afro-Americans—History—1877–1964.   I. Title.
II. Series.
E444.B9   1996
305.5'67'092—dc 20
[B]
96-9626   CIP

Originally published in 1895 by P. Anstadt & Sons, York, Pennsylvania. This
Bison Books edition follows the original in beginning chapter 1 on arabic
page 11; no material has been omitted.

INTRODUCTION TO THE BISON BOOKS EDITION

Willard B. Gatewood

The emergence of a virulent form of racism in the 1890s confronted the nation's African Americans with a crisis of major proportions. The economic depression, social dislocation, and political turmoil during the decade created a climate in which racial demagoguery flourished. Mired in poverty and confronted by increasing incidents of intimidation and violence, black citizens were powerless to defeat either efforts to disfranchise them in the South or to thwart the proliferation of racially discriminatory practices elsewhere. Fearful of being stripped of virtually all rights and privileges of citizenship, African Americans responded to the crisis of the 1890s in numerous editorials, sermons, speeches, and books which ranged in tone from militant outrage to accommodationism. Though not technically a part of the response to the violence and proscriptions facing black citizens, the life histories of former slaves that appeared at the same time spoke to issues relevant to their plight and outlined strategies for their survival. As chronicles of "upward struggles," these works documented how far African Americans had progressed since Emancipation and indicated, sometimes with great subtlety, how much more they could achieve and contribute to the nation if relieved of legal and extralegal barriers.

Among the African Americans whose autobiographies appeared in the troubled decade was that of Henry Clay Bruce[1] who related his experiences as a slave and as a free man in the belief that they offered a formula by which blacks could safely navigate the uncertain terrain of the 1890s and succeed "in the race of life as newly made citizens." His *The New Man: Twenty-Nine Years a Slave, Twenty-Nine Years a Free Man* appeared in 1895, shortly before his friend and hero, Booker T. Washington, delivered his famous "Atlanta Compromise" address in which he urged African Americans to focus their energies on acquiring marketable skills and property rather than on securing civil and political rights. The themes of the Atlanta speech appeared in more elaborate form in the two versions of his autobiography, *The Story of My Life and Work* (1900) and *Up from Slavery* (1901).

In many respects the autobiographies and philosophies of Bruce and Washington were similar. Both autobiographies were narratives of ascent—success stories—in the tradition of slave narratives in which ascent referred to escaping slavery and arriving safely in a free state. The life-histories of Bruce and Washington also described a different kind of ascent, one that chronicled how two individuals transcended poverty and prejudice to rise far above their origins. No less than Washington's *Up from Slavery*, Bruce's narrative extolled self-reliance and perseverance, exuded optimism and self-confidence, and exhibited strong racial pride. While both provided ample evidence of the role of antiblack prejudice in obstructing the progress of African Americans, they nonetheless were generous in their assessments of whites who had assisted blacks before and after Emancipation. Even though Bruce was less direct than Washington in embracing an accommodationist philosophy, he too knew the fine points of racial etiquette and practiced diplomacy with consummate skill. He discouraged expressions of outrage and militant actions by blacks, however justifiable they may have been, on the grounds that such responses were counterproductive. Rather, he counseled patience and the quiet acquisition of education and wealth. Both Bruce and Washington found in their own careers ample justification for such advice.

Despite similarities in form and message, the autobiographies of Bruce and Washington exhibit significant differences. Some resulted from the disparities in their ages, length of servitude, and experiences in the slave system. Born in 1856, Washington was a slave for his first nine years and therefore experienced slavery only as a child. In contrast, Bruce was a slave for his first twenty-nine years, which meant that he possessed first-hand knowledge of changes in the meaning and demands of slavery as one matured into an adult. Like Washington, he recalled a happy, relatively carefree childhood, but as a youth and man he suffered indignities largely unknown to children. The experiences of the two men also differed in one other respect: Washington remained in Virginia throughout his life as a slave, while Bruce was exposed to a succession of masters and to the different varieties of slavery that existed in three distinct areas of the country.

Henry Clay Bruce was born in 1836 on a plantation owned by Lemuel Bruce and located in Prince Edward County, Virginia, near the town of Farmville. This piedmont area of south-central Virginia produced abundant crops of tobacco, wheat, corn, and oats. A prosperous farmer who was a member of an old and well-known family, Lemuel Bruce owned two families of slaves. When he died, his son, William B., inherited one family and his daughter, Rebecca, the other that bore the name Bruce. For reasons that are unclear, Henry Clay Bruce's father (who receives one brief mention in the autobiography) was separated from his family in the division of slaves at the death of their owner, leaving his mother, Polly, the head of the black Bruce family. Polly Bruce, who was clearly the dominant influence in her son's early life, had a total of eleven children, some of whom, including Henry Clay and his younger brother Blanche Kelso,[2] were obviously of mixed ancestry. When Rebecca Bruce married Pettus (spelled Pettis in the autobiography) Perkinson, the black Bruces became a part of Perkinson's plantation, also located in Prince Edward County, except for several of Polly's children who had either been acquired by or allowed to remain with their former master's son, William B. Bruce.

The death of Rebecca Bruce Perkinson a little more than a year after her marriage plunged her husband into a state of deep despondency that apparently prompted a restlessness from which he seems never to have recovered. Increasingly dissatisfied with his plantation in Virginia and its worn-out soil, Pettus Perkinson decided to migrate to Missouri where his brother and brother-in-law had already settled. By the 1840s many upper-South planters had begun to move to the West or Southwest, but few equaled the wanderlust of Perkinson who transferred his place of residence four times within six years—from Virginia to Missouri in 1844, back to Virginia three years later, then to the vicinity of Holly Springs, Mississippi, in 1849, and finally back to Missouri the following year. Only the strong objections of his slaves, including young Bruce and his brothers, persuaded Perkinson later to abandon plans to move to Texas.

Unlike most slaves, Bruce not only moved often and lived under a variety of conditions, but he was regularly "hired out" and worked for masters other than his owner. In Mississippi he was "hired out" to pick cotton and in Missouri to work in tobacco factories and at various other jobs. Since the Bruce slave family, known as the "Bruce hands," were in great demand because of their industriousness, their owner was able to demand high wages for their labor. Bruce's autobiography not only provides valuable insight into the different work routines under which he labored, but it also includes assessments of the various masters to whom he was "hired out," classifying them according to the degree of humanity they displayed in their treatment of bondsmen. Always careful to avoid conveying the impression that all masters were inhumane, Bruce concluded that "slave owners, even Mississippians, were not all brutal." He frankly admitted, too, that some slaves were lazy, trifling, and inclined to resist authority, but maintained that good masters "made good slaves with few exceptions."

Until the Civil War, the history of the black Bruces was intertwined with that of two white families, the Bruces and Perkinsons. Henry Clay Bruce's mother, who was at one time or another the cook in the households of both families, functioned as surrogate mother to William B. "Willie" Perkinson, the young son of her widowed owner. Bruce himself served as "playmate and guardian" of Willie until he was succeeded in that capacity by his younger brother Blanche K. Bruce, who may have been the natural son of the elder Perkinson and hence Willie's half-brother. At any rate, the black Bruce brothers acquired the rudiments of education from Willie Perkinson, who shared his "lessons" with them.

Like many other slave parents, Polly Bruce possessed a profound reverence for learning. The "desire to learn" was, in her son's words, a "trait of character" that ran through her family. Although Polly Bruce remained illiterate, she was determined that her children would at least learn to read. She saw to it that as one child learned the alphabet, he or she would teach another, so that by the beginning of the Civil War all the Bruce children could read and some could write. That the slave family was able to achieve a degree of literacy owed much to the indulgence of their owner and to the environment that prevailed in the area of Missouri where the Bruces lived. In the early 1850s whites in Charitan and Carroll counties, Missouri, unlike those in Virginia, manifested little opposition to slaves learning to read and write. Bruce recalled that in Missouri he could buy any book he wanted if he "had the money to pay for it."

The relative lack of restraints on slave education in Missouri was only one reason why Bruce preferred the state to either Virginia or Mississippi. He considered the slaves in north-central Missouri counties where he lived as infinitely more intelligent and better educated than those he had known "in the more extreme southern states." He was repelled by the latter's superstitions and practice of voodoo, which he described as by-products of their benightedness and which made them easy prey to all kinds of deception that often relieved them of their few valuables. That the slaves in north-central Missouri rebuffed the so-called conjurors from the Deep South convinced Bruce of their superior "intelligence."

Late in the 1850s when Pettus Perkinson began developing a farm near Brunswick, Missouri, Bruce became his foreman and in effect managed the entire farming operation. The position of foreman placed on him more responsibility but also allowed a greater degree of freedom. Such freedom increased with the outbreak of the Civil War until Bruce, though still technically a slave, felt few restraints on his activities and movements. From the peculiar perspective of Missouri, he observed the progress of the war and felt keenly the sharp divisions between Confederate and Union sympathizers among the state's white population. Having persuaded a slave girl on a neighboring plantation to become his wife, Bruce decided to flee to freedom in neighboring Kansas. He and his fiancée began their flight on March 30, 1864; crossed the Missouri River to Leavenworth, Kansas; and on the next day were married by a minister of the African Methodist Episcopal church. Not until Bruce was on Kansas soil did he consider himself a truly free man.

Once in Leavenworth, the Bruces immediately secured jobs and moved into a two-room house. The duplicity of a white man thwarted their first effort to become homeowners and cheated them out of a sizable down payment. This experience convinced Bruce that Missouri slaveowners were far more honest in dealings with African Americans than were whites in the free state of Kansas. But neither his aborted effort to purchase a home nor the antiblack prejudice invoked by Irish laborers in Leavenworth to squeeze African Americans out of the local job market lessened his determination to achieve economic security and independence. Within a few years he managed to save enough money to establish a small business: he opened a store in a rented building located near the levee in Leavenworth. When fire destroyed the building along with his stock, he secured the assistance of a white wholesale liquor dealer to reopen his store in another location.

After almost six years in Leavenworth, Bruce decided to move up the Missouri River to Atchison, Kansas, where opportunities apparently appeared more promising. In Atchison he opened another store in 1870, and five years later his inventory was again destroyed by fire. For the fourth time within a decade he opened yet another store, but this time in a brick structure. When a shortage of funds forced him out of business in 1878, he managed to borrow enough money to purchase two express teams with which he made a modest living for his wife and four young children.

Bruce, despite his economic setbacks, appears to have been conspicuous in Atchison's black community. Having followed the fortunes of the Republican party since the presidential election of 1856, he became active in local Republican politics and received the party's nomination for the lower house of the Kansas legislature in 1880. In a close race with a white Democrat, George W. Glick, who later became governor (1883–85), Bruce lost the election by twenty-five votes. Not only had he exhausted his financial resources in his unsuccessful bid for political office but income from his express business also virtually ceased during the severe winter of 1880–81. Fortunately for Bruce, his politically influential friends secured for him appointment as doorkeeper of the Kansas Senate which paid a weekly salary of twenty-one dollars, an income that enabled him and his family to survive the winter. After the legislature adjourned and his job as Senate doorkeeper came to an end, he signed on as the foreman of a railroad construction crew and held that job until late in the summer of 1881 when a telegram from his younger brother, Blanche K. Bruce, brought news that would improve his economic condition and remove him permanently from Kansas.

During slavery Henry Clay Bruce had often intervened to protect his younger brother, Blanche, who in 1881 was in a position to repay him. After a brief sojourn in Kansas, Blanche Bruce settled in Mississippi in 1868, where he prospered as a cotton planter and rose rapidly in the Republican party ranks during Reconstruction. Elected to the United States Senate in 1874, he became the first African American to serve a full six-year term in that body. Defeated for reelection in 1880 because the Democrats had "redeemed" Mississippi, Bruce remained in Washington, established an insurance, loan, and real estate agency, and received a succession of important federal appointments from Republican presidents. The first of these was his appointment as Register of Treasury (1881–85). A man of means and considerable influence, Register Bruce secured his impoverished brother in Kansas a clerkship in the Post Office Department in August 1881.

After a year in this position, Henry Clay Bruce was appointed, again through the influence of his brother, as an examiner in the Pension Office in the Interior Department. He was aware of this debt to his younger brother and paid homage to him in a revealing passage in his autobiography. "My younger brother, B. K. Bruce (now ex-Senator)," he wrote, "had succeeded me as playmate and guardian of Willie

[Perkinson], and being anxious to learn, soon caught up with me and by Willie's aid went ahead of me and has held his place during all these years since." Throughout his later life, Henry Clay Bruce was usually identified as the senator's brother.

Bruce spent the last two decades of his life in Washington. That he retained his position in the Pension Office under both Republican and Democratic presidents and received several promotions suggested that his performance and skill as a pension examiner were sufficiently impressive to merit the respect of superiors regardless of their party affiliation. During his tenure in Washington, Bruce and his family rarely received notice in the social columns of the local black press and certainly did not possess the elevated status of his brother, the former senator, and his wife, who stood at the pinnacle of the city's black social life. Nevertheless, as a respected government employee and the brother of one of the best-known African Americans in the country, Bruce was assured a place among what he termed "the better class of people," a group that included teachers, professionals, government clerks, and a few others in Washington's African-American community. His membership in and devotion to the Fifteenth Street Presbyterian Church, an old and prestigious black congregation, suggested that he and his family were considered members of the social group he admired.

Despite its subtitle, Bruce's autobiography does not devote equal attention to his life as a slave and as a free man. His twenty-nine years as a slave receive far more extensive treatment. Even though this portion of his narrative provides graphic details about his various work experiences and what he considered dramatic incidents, it either omits altogether or is lacking in specificity about some matters of significance, especially those regarding his family. For example, his brief references to his wife and single reference to his children reveal little, not even their names. Other than his famous brother Blanche K. Bruce, there are only allusions to most of his other nine siblings, especially his three sisters; his two older brothers, James and Calvin, receive only passing notice. In view of his tendency to digress, move back and forth chronologically, and emphasize education, it appears curious that he omitted any mention of James's son and his nephew, Blanche K. Bruce, the namesake of his uncle and the first black graduate of the University of Kansas (1885), who had become a well-known educator in Kansas well before the publication of *The New Man*.

The portion of Bruce's autobiography devoted to his twenty-nine years as a free man is at best sketchy on his personal life. It consists largely of his observations on the post-Emancipation progress and problems of black citizens and his advice on overcoming what he considered obstacles to the advancement of the race. While the autobiography provides lengthy assessments of the various Commissioners of Pensions under whom Bruce had served by 1895, it virtually ignores Washington's black community and his role in it.

Even more surprising, perhaps, was Bruce's failure to address directly the issue of the Exodusters, the southern blacks who poured into Kansas during his final years there. It seems doubtful, however, that he agreed with his brother Blanche, who forthrightly opposed the large-scale migration of blacks out of the South, known as the Exodus of 1879–80, especially in view of his sympathy for the black southerners who migrated to Kansas earlier during and immediately after the Civil War. Bruce expressed his hostility toward the free blacks, the "freeborns," in Kansas who considered themselves superior to the ex-slave migrants and sought to exclude them from their social circle and reserve all "the fat places" in politics, churches, and fraternal orders for themselves. Bruce defended the freedmen and castigated the pretentious freeborns as "old fogies and leeches."

The ideas on race and the needs of blacks that appeared in *The New Man* included themes that Bruce had articulated earlier. For example, his discourses on the importance of education to African Americans in his autobiography closely resembled those he had expressed in a widely publicized speech before the Colored State Convention in Topeka in 1880.[3] In that address he insisted that if blacks were to enjoy freedom and prosperity, they had to become educated and rid themselves of superstitions. "An ignorant race," he declared in Topeka, "can not succeed in this country." Disavowing any hostility toward organized religion, he nonetheless warned that the disproportionate number of young African Americans enrolled in higher education with the aim of becoming ministers would only reinforce the race's preoccupation with the hereafter and things of the spirit, leaving unaddressed the economic and social realities that faced the masses. "I believe," he said, "in preparing to live as well as die." Convinced that "money and education are the two great levers that move the world," he argued that blacks needed schooling that would provide them with marketable skills and produce businessmen far more than they needed additional ministers of the gospel, who often mixed religion with politics for self-advancement and failed to provide constructive leadership. He subscribed to Booker T. Washington's education recipe of industrial or vocational schools for rank-and-file blacks. The wealth and respectability that would result from such education would ultimately ensure African Americans their "rightful place in the esteem and confidence of the nation."

That Bruce's race consciousness is evident throughout his autobiography is scarcely surprising. A man of great dignity, who even as a slave resisted, at substantial personal risks, what he considered assaults on his self-respect, Bruce extolled the virtues of African Americans in general, describing them as industrious workers, patriotic and law-abiding citizens, and loyal and brave soldiers, a people worthy of being accorded the privileges of first-class citizenship. In his view they were far superior to the "herd of ignorant and lawless foreigners," the New Immigrants who poured into the country beginning in the late nineteenth century, bringing alien ideas and attempting to exclude blacks from the labor market.

Notwithstanding his race consciousness, Bruce clearly considered class more important and relevant to the crisis confronting African Americans. No other theme appeared so frequently in *The New Man*. The "hydra-headed monster" of prejudice against blacks, he argued, was not so much "due to our color as to our condition"; that is, to the prevalence of poverty and ignorance among African Americans. In his discussion of class he referred repeatedly to the significance of the quality of one's "blood" and spoke in terms of superior and inferior blood. While it is not always clear what he meant by blood quality, it appears that superior blood was equated with "clean character," industriousness, self-confidence, and other traits which he associated with "the better classes" and "aristocrats," those people who had "made our country what it is today—the best government on the face of the globe." In his view, those Americans who were immoral, lazy, ignorant, and "degraded" obviously had inferior blood "in their veins." Though convinced that "blood will tell," Bruce did not believe that superior blood was the exclusive preserve of whites any more than inferior blood belonged only to blacks; rather, he insisted that the manifestations of the two kinds of blood were found among both races. There were "high-toned" whites and blacks who existed alongside "poor white trash" and "degraded" blacks.

In his analyses of white and black classes, Bruce clearly identified with the "better classes" of both races, those people whom he believed to be the keys to African-American progress. He held poor whites and those blacks who were "shiftless, worthless, and thoroughly degraded" responsible for the backwardness of the South and for the plight of African Americans in general. Whether describing the poor whites before or after the Civil War in his autobiography, Bruce expressed his low opinion of them and accused them of being the principal perpetrators of mischief against blacks. His primary criticism of his owner, Pettus Perkinson, whom he generally held in high regard, was Perkinson's penchant for associating with poor whites, even allowing them to dine at his table. Bruce counseled African Americans to follow his example by casting their lot with the white upper class and to avoid alliances with native-born "white trash" or ignorant foreigners who together made up the dregs of society. Like some other African Americans, Bruce tied his star to the so-called white aristocrats at precisely the time that their power in the South was being eroded by the rise of racial demagogues, and the Mississippi Way of race relations was increasingly becoming the American Way.

If Bruce was harsh in his assessment of poor whites, he was scarcely less so in regard to those African Americans who occupied the lowest rung in the black class structure. While he was convinced that this element contributed significantly to the problem of blacks in general, he took pains to explain that blacks with "inferior blood" no more represented their race than poor "white trash" represented all whites. In an effort to combat the white notion that blacks constituted an undifferentiated mass, he traced the evolution of the black class structure. Even in slavery, he pointed out, there was a black elite made up of "high-toned slaves" who refused to succumb to "abject servility," held their heads high, and lived virtuous, upright lives insofar as conditions permitted. From their ranks, he argued, came the post–Civil War black leaders. By the 1890s, the black class structure, as he described it, consisted of "three distinct grades": at the top were those wealthy enough to maintain a lifestyle comparable to upper class whites; in the middle were the respectable business people, professionals, tradesmen, and laborers; at the bottom was the immoral, criminal element that Bruce chastised whites for using as the sole criterion for judging all African Americans.

Bruce's personal life in Washington, no less than his musings about "blood" and "distinct grades" in his autobiography, testified to his class consciousness. Careful to avoid all association with "second class people" of both races, he appeared to be an exemplary practitioner of the genteel performance that characterized Washington's black upper class. The decorum, self-restraint, and respectability evident in his conduct, manner, and even his dress assured him a place among "the better class" of people within the black community as well as the respect of whites of comparable status.

In 1902, seven years after the publication of *The New Man*, Bruce was still at his post in the Pension Office and was busy at work on another book. The nature of this work is not known, but it may well have been designed to augment the sketchy account that the autobiography provided of his life in Kansas and Washington, D.C. Late in the summer of 1902 he suddenly became ill and died less than two weeks later. A large crowd attended his funeral at the Fifteenth Street Presbyterian Church to pay their respects to, in the words of an African-American editor, "one of the most enterprising men of the Negro race."[4]

NOTES

1. The autobiography is the source of most data on Henry Clay Bruce. The brief sketch of his life in J. H. Johnston, *They Came This Way* (Leavenworth: J. H. Johnston, 1988), 105–13, is based almost entirely on the autobiography. Much more has been written about Blanche K. Bruce, his brother, and these works contain valuable information on the Bruce family. See especially William C. Harris, "Blanche K. Bruce of Mississippi: Conservative Assimilationist," in *Southern Black Leaders of the Reconstruction Era*, edited by Howard W. Rabinowitz (Urbana: University of Illinois Press, 1982), 3–38; Melvin I. Urofsky, "Blanche K. Bruce: United States Senator, 1875–1881," *Journal of Mississippi History*, 29 (May 1967): 118–41; Sadie Daniel St. Clair, "The National Career of Blanche Kelso Bruce," (Ph.D. diss., New York University, 1947); and Williard B. Gatewood, *Aristocrats of Color: The Black Elite, 1880–1920* (Bloomington: Indiana University Press, 1990). Other works consulted include Herbert C. Bradshaw, *History of Prince Edward County, Virginia* (Richmond: Dietz Press, 1955); Harrison A. Trexler, *Slavery in Missouri, 1804–1865* (Baltimore: Johns Hopkins Press, 1914); Richard B. Sheridan, "From Slavery in Missouri to Freedom in Kansas; The Influx of Black Fugitives and Contrabands in Kansas, 1854–1865, *Kansas History*, 12 (spring 1989): 28–47; *Appleton's Annual Cyclopedia of Important Events for the Year 1880* (New York: D. Appleton and Company, 1883); and Nell Irvin Painter, *Exodusters: Black Migration to Kansas after Reconstruction* (New York: W. W. Norton, 1896).

2. William C. Harris writes: "Born with the surname Branch, he [Blanche

K. Bruce] assumed the name Bruce, the name of his mother's master, after he freed himself during the Civil War." Although Prince Edward County included a large and prominent family by the name Branch, Henry Clay Bruce made no mention of them or of changing his name from Branch to Bruce. See Harris, "Blanche K. Bruce of Mississippi," 33n.

3. For Bruce's speech, see *Herald of Kansas* (Topeka), May 14, 1880.

4. *Washington Bee*, September 6, 1902.

PREFACE.

The author offers to the public this little book, containing his personal recollections of slavery, with the modest hope that it will be found to present an impartial and unprejudiced view of that system. His experience taught him that all masters were not cruel, and that all slaves were not maltreated. There were brutal masters and there were mean, trifling lazy slaves. While some masters cruelly whipped, half fed and overworked their slaves, there were many others who provided for their slaves with fatherly care, saw that they were well fed and clothed, and would neither whip them themselves, nor permit others to do so.

Having reached the age of twenty-nine before he could call himself a free man, and having been peculiarly fortunate in all his surroundings during the period of his slavery, the author considers himself competent to deal with all concerned, fairly and without prejudice, and he will feel more than repaid for his labor, if he can throw even some little new light upon this much mooted question. He believes that we are too far removed now from the heart burnings and cruelties of that system of slavery, horrible as it was, and too far removed from that bloody strife that destroyed the system, root and branch, to let our accounts of it now be colored by its memories. Freedom has been sweet indeed to the ex-bondman. It has been one glorious harvest of good things, and he fervently prays for grace to forget the past and for strength to go forward to resolutely meet the future.

The author early became impressed with the belief, which has since settled into deep conviction, that just as the whites were divided into two great classes, so the slaves were divided. There are certain characteristics of good blood, that manifest themselves in the honor and ability and other virtues of their possessors, and these virtues could be seen as often exemplified beneath black skins as beneath white ones. There were those slaves who would have suffered death rather than submit to dishonor; who, though they knew they suffered a great wrong in their enslavement, gave their best services to their masters, realizing, philosophically, that the wisest course was to make the best of their unfortunate situation. They would not submit to punishment, but would fight or run away rather than be whipped.

On the other hand there was a class of Negroes among the slaves who were lazy and mean. They were as untrue to their fellows as to themselves. Like the poor whites to whom they were analogous in point of blood, they had little or no honor, no high sense of duty, little or no appreciation of the domestic virtues, and since their emancipation, both of these inferior blooded classes have been content to grovel in the mire of degradation.

The "poor white" class was held in slavery, just as real as the blacks, and their degradation was all the more condemnable, because being white, all the world was open to them, yet they *from choice*, remained in the South, in this position of *quasi* slavery.

During the slave days these poor whites seemed to live for no higher purpose than to spy on the slaves, and to lie on them. Their ambitions were gratified if they could be overseers, or slave drivers, or "padrollers" as the slaves called them. This class was conceived and born of a poor blood, whose inferiority linked its members for all time to things mean and low. They were the natural enemies of the slaves, and to this day they have sought to belittle and humiliate the ambitious freeman, by the long catalogue of laws framed with the avowed intention of robbing him of his manhood rights. It is they who cry out about "social equality," knowing full well, that the high-toned Negro would not associate with him if he could.

If there had been no superior blooded class of blacks in the South, during the dark and uncertain days of the war, there would not have been the history of that band of noble selfsacrificing heroes, who guarded with untiring and unquestioned faith, the homes and honor of the families of the very men who were fighting to tighten their chains. No brighter pages of history will ever be written, than those which record the services of the slaves, who were left in charge of their masters' homes. These men will be found in every case to have been those, who as slaves would not be whipped, nor suffer punishment; who would protect the honor of their own women at any cost; but who would work with honesty and fidelity at any task imposed upon them.

The author's recollections begin with the year 1842, and he will endeavor to show how slaves were reared and treated as he saw it. His recollections will include something of the industrial conditions amidst which he was reared. He will discuss from the standpoint of the slave, the conditions which led to the war, his status during the war, and will record his experiences and observations regarding the progress of the Negro since emancipation.

It is his belief, that one of the most stupendous of the wrongs which the Negro has suffered, was in turning the whole army of slaves loose in a hostile country, without money, without friends, without experience in home getting or even self-support. Their two hundred and fifty years of unrequited labor counted for naught. They were free but penniless in the land which they had made rich.

But though they were robbed of the reward of their labor, though they have been denied their common rights, though they have been discriminated against in every walk of life and in favor of every breed of foreign anarchist and socialist, though they have been made to feel the measured hate of the poor white man's venom, yet through it all they have been true; true to the country they *owe* (?) so little, true to the flag that denies them protection, true to the government that practically disowns them, true to their honor, fidelity and loyalty, the birthrights of superior blood.

H. C. BRUCE,
WASHINGTON, D. C.

TABLE OF CONTENTS.

CHAPTER I.

CHAPTER I.

My mother often told me that I was born, March 3rd, of the year that Martin Van Buren was elected President of the United States, and I have therefore always regarded March 3rd, 1836, as the date of my birth. Those who are familiar with the customs that obtained at the South in the days of slavery, will readily understand why so few of the ex-slaves can give the correct date of their birth, for, being uneducated, they were unable to keep records themselves, and their masters, having no special interest in the matter, saw no necessity for such records. So that the slave parents, in order to approximate the birth of a child, usually associated it with the occurrence of some important event, such, for instance, as " the year the stars fell," (1833), the death of some prominent man, the marriage of one of the master's children, or some notable historical event. Thus by recalling any one of these occurrences, the age of their own children was determined. Not being able to read and write, they were compelled to resort to the next best thing within reach, memory, the only diary in which the records of their marriages, births and deaths were registered, and which was also the means by which their mathematical problems were solved, their accounts kept, when they had any to keep.

Of course there were thousands of such cases as
E. M. Dillard's, the one which I shall mention, but as
his case will represent theirs, I will speak of his only.
He was an intimate acquaintance of mine, a man born
a slave, freed by the emancipation proclamation when
over thirty years old, without even a knowledge of the
alphabet, but he had a practical knowledge of men and
business matters, which enabled him to acquire a com-
fortable living, a nice home, to educate his children and
conduct a small business of his own.   But the greatest
wonder about this man was the exactness and correct
business way in which he conducted it in buying and
selling, and especially in casting up accounts, seemingly
with care, accuracy, and rapidity as any educated man
could have done.   But it was the result of a good
memory and a full share of brain.

The memories of slaves were simply wonderful.
They were not unmindful, nor indifferent as to occurrences of interest transpiring around them, but as the
principal medium through which we obtain information
was entirely closed to them, of course their knowledge
of matters and things must necessarily have been confined within a very narrow limit; but when anything of
importance transpired within their knowledge, they
knowing the date thereof, could, by reference to it as a
basis, approximate the date of some other event in
question.   Then there were a great many old men
among them that might be called sages, men who knew
the number of days in each month, in each year, could

tell the exact date when Easter and Whit Sunday would come, because most masters gave Monday following each of these Sundays as a holiday to slaves.

These old sages determined dates by means of straight marks and notches, made on a long stick with a knife, and were quite accurate in arriving at correct dates. I have often seen the sticks upon which they kept their records, but failed to understand the system upon which they based their calculations, yet I found them eminently correct. It was too intricate for me.

My parents belonged to Lemuel Bruce, who died about the year 1836, leaving two children, William Bruce and Rebecca Bruce, who went to live with their aunt, Mrs. Prudence Perkinson; he also left two families of slaves, and they were divided between his two children; my mother's family fell to Miss Rebecca, and the other family, the head of which was known as Bristo, was left to William B. Bruce. Then it was that family ties were broken, the slaves were all hired out, my mother to one man and my father to another. I was too young then to know anything about it, and have to rely entirely on what I have heard my mother and others older than myself say.

My personal recollections go back to the year 1841, when my mother was hired to a lady, Mrs. Ludy Waddel by name. Miss Rebecca Bruce married Mr. Pettis Perkinson, and soon after her slaves were taken to their new home, then known as the Rowlett Place, at which point we began a new life. It is but simple justice to Mr. Perkinson to say, that though springing from a family known in that part of the country as hard task-masters, he was himself a, kind and considerate man.   His father had given him some ten or twelve slaves, among whom were two boys about my own age. As we were quite young, we were tenderly treated.

To state that slave children under thirteen years of age were tenderly treated probably requires further explanation.   During the crop season in Virginia, slave men and women worked in the fields daily, and such females as had sucklings were allowed to come to them three times a day between sun rise and sun set, for the purpose of nursing their babes, who were left in the care of an old woman, who was assigned to the care of these children because she was too old or too feeble for field work.   Such old women usually had to care for, and prepare the meals of all children under working age.   They were furnished with plenty of good, wholesome food by the master, who took special care to see that it was properly cooked and served to them as often as they desired it.

On very large plantations there were many such old women, who spent the remainder of their lives caring for children of younger women.   Masters took great pride in their gangs of young slaves, especially when they looked " fat and sassy," and would often have them come to the great house yard to play, particularly when they had visitors.   Freed from books and mental worry of all kinds, and having all the outdoor exercise they wanted, the slave children had nothing to do but eat, play and grow, and physically speaking, attain to good size and height, which was the special wish and aim of their masters, because a tall, well-proportioned slave man or woman, in case of a sale, would always command the highest price paid. So then it is quite plain, that it was not only the master's pride, but his financial interest as well, to have these children enjoy every comfort possible, which would aid in their physical make up, and to see to it that they were tenderly treated.

But Mr. Perkinson's wife lived but a short time, dying in 1842. She left one child, William E. Perkinson, known in his later life as Judge W. E. Perkinson, of Brunswick, Missouri. Mr. Perkinson built a new house for himself, " The great house," and quarters for his slaves on his own land, near what is now known as Green Bay, Prince Edward County, Virginia. But I don't think that Mrs. Perkinson lived to occupy the new house. My mother was assigned to a cabin at the new place during the spring of 1842. But after the death of his young wife, Mr. Perkinson became greatly dissatisfied with his home and its surroundings, showing that all that was dear to him was gone, and that he longed for a change, and being persuaded by his brother-in-law, W. B. Bruce, who was preparing to go to the western country, as Missouri and Kentucky were then called, he dicided to break up his Virginia home, and take his slaves to Missouri, in company with Mr. W. B. Bruce.

The time to start was agreed upon, and those old enough to work were given a long holiday from January to April, 1844, when we left our old Virginia home, bound for Chariton County, Missouri. In this event there were no separations of husbands and wives, because of the fact that my father and Bristo were both dead, and they were the only married men in the Bruce family.

Among the slaves that were given to Mr. Perkinson by his father was only one marrried man, uncle Watt, as we called him, and he and his wife and children were carried along with the rest of us.

I shall never forget the great preparations made for our start to the West There were three large wagons in the outfit, one for the whites and two for the slaves. The whites in the party were Messrs. Perkinson, Bruce, Samuel Wooten, and James Dorsell. The line of march was struck early in April, 1844. I remember that I was delighted with the beautiful sceneries, towns, rivers, people in their different styles of costumes, and so many strange things that I saw on that trip from our old home to Louisville. But the most wonderful experience to me was, when we took a steamer at Louisville for St. Louis. The idea of a house floating on the water was a new one to me, at least, and I doubt very much whether any of the white men of the party had ever seen a steamboat before.

I am unable to recall the route, and the many sights, and incidents of that long trip of nearly fifteen hundred miles, and shall not attempt to describe it. But finally we reached our destination, which was the home of Jack Perkinson, brother of Mr. Pettis Perkinson, about June or July, 1844. His place was located about seven or eight miles from Keytesville, Missouri. At that time this country was sparsely settled ; a farm house could be only seen in every eight or ten miles. I was greatly pleased with the country, for there was plenty of everything to live on, game, fish, wild fruits, and berries. The only drawback to our pleasure was Jack Perkinson, who was the meanest man I had ever seen. He had about thirty-five slaves on his large farm and could and did raise more noise, do more thrashing of men, women and children, than any other man in that county.

Our folks were soon hired out to work in the tobacco factories at Keytesville, except the old women, and such children as were too small to be put to work. I was left at this place with my mother and her younger children and was happy. I was too young to be put to work, and there being on the farm four or five boys about my age, spent my time with them hunting and fishing. There was a creek near by in which we caught plenty of fish. We made lines of hemp grown on the farm and hooks of bent pins. When we got a bite, up went the pole and quite often the fish, eight or ten feet in the air. We never waited for what is called a good bite, for if we did the fish would get the bait and escape capture, or get off when hooked if not thrown quickly upon the land. But fish then were very plentiful and not as scary as now The hardest job with us was digging bait.   We often brought home as much as five pounds of fish in a day.

There was game in abundance, but our hunting was always for young rabbits and squirrels, and we hunted them with hounds brought with us from Virginia.   I had never before seen so many squirrels. The trees there were usually small and too far apart for them to jump from tree to tree, and when we saw one "treed" by the dogs, one of us climbed up and forced it to jump, and when it did, in nine cases out of ten the dogs would catch it.   We often got six or eight in a day's hunting.

Another sport which we enjoyed was gathering the eggs of prairie chickens.   On account of the danger of snake bites, we were somewhat restricted in the pursuit of this pleasure, being forbidden to go far away from the cabins.   Their eggs were not quite as large as the domestic hen's, but are of a very fine flavor.

North of Jack Perkinson's farm was a great expanse of prairie four or five miles wide and probably twenty or thirty long—indeed it might have been fifty miles long.   There were a great many snakes of various sizes and kinds, but the most dangerous and the one most dreaded was the rattlesnake, whose bite was almost certain death in those days, but for which now the doctors have found so many cures that we seldom hear of a death from that cause.   When allowed to go or when we could steal away, which we very often did, we usually took a good sized basket and found eggs enough to fill it before returning.   We saw a great many snakes, killing some and passing others by, especially the large ones.   There were thousands of prairie chickens scattered over this plain, and eggs were easily found.   One thing was in our favor ; these wild chickens never selected very tall grass for nests. But it almost makes me shudder now, when I think of it, and remember that we were barefooted at the time, with reptiles on every side, some of which would crawl away or into their holes while others would show fight. But none of us were bitten by them.   On these prairies large herds of deer could be seen in almost any direction.   I have seen as many as one hundred together. Jack Perkinson was not a hunter, kept no gun, and of course we had none, so we could not get any deer. There were a great many wolves around that place and I stood in mortal fear of them, but never had any encounter with one.   They usually prowled about at night and kept the young slave men from going to balls or parties

The most vicious wild animal I met or encountered was the hog.   There were a great many of them around the farm, especially in the timber south of it. In that timber were some very large hickory nuts—the finest I ever saw.   I remember one occasion when we were out gathering nuts, having our dogs with us. They went a short distance from us, but very soon we heard them barking and saw them running toward us followed by a drove of wild hogs in close proximity. We hardly had time to climb trees for safety.   I was so closely pressed that an old boar caught my foot, pulling off the shoe, but I held on to the limb of the tree and climbed out of danger, although minus my shoe.   One minute later and I would not have been here to pen these lines, for those hogs would have torn and eaten me in short order.   From my safe position in the tree I looked down on those vicious wild animals tearing up my shoe. We had escaped immediate death, but were greatly frightened because the hogs lay down under the trees and night was coming on. We had shouted for help but could not make ourselves heard. Every time our dogs came near, some big boar would chase them away and come back to the drove. We reasoned together, and came to the conclusion that if we would drive the dogs farther away the hogs would leave. Being up trees we could see our dogs for some distance away and we drove them back. After a while the hogs seemed to have forgotten us. A few large ones got up, commenced rooting and grunting, and soon the drove moved on. When they had gotten a hundred yards away we slid down, and then such a race for the fence and home. It was a close call. But we kept that little fun mum, for if Jack Perkinson had learned of his narrow escape from the loss of two or three Negro boys worth five or six hundred dollars each, he would have given us a severe whipping.

About January 1, 1845, my mother and her children, including myself and those younger, were hired to one James Means, a brickmaker, living near Huntsville, Randolph County, Missouri. I remember the day when he came after us with a two-horse team. He had several children, the eldest being a boy Although Cyrus was a year older than I, he could not lick me. He and I had to feed the stock and haul trees to be cut into wood for fire, which his father had felled in the timber. Mr. Means also owned a girl about fourteen years old called Cat, and as soon as spring came he commenced work on the brick yard with Cat and me as off bearers. This, being my first real work, was fun for a while, but soon became very hard and I got whipped nearly every day, not because I did not work, but because I could not stand it. Having to carry a double mold all day long in the hot sun I broke down. Finally Mr. Means made for my special benefit two single molds, and after that I received no more punishment from him.

Mr. Perkinson soon became disgusted with Missouri, and leaving his slaves in the care of W. B. Bruce to be hired out yearly, went back to Virginia. Some said it was a widow, Mrs. Wooten, who took him back, while others believed that it was because he could not stand the cursing and whipping of slaves carried on by his brother Jack whom he could not control. This man, Jack Perkinson, died about the year 1846, and left a wife and three children. Although he had borne the reputation of being the hardest master in that county, his wife was quite different. When she took charge of the estate, she hired out the slaves, most of them to the tobacco factory owners, and really received more money yearly for them than when they worked upon the farm. After her death the estate passed to her children and was managed by the eldest son, Pettis, who was very kind to his slaves until they became free by the Emancipation Proclamation. I am informed that the very best of friendship still exists between the whites and blacks of that family.

In January, 1846, with my older brothers I was hired to Judge Applegate, who conducted a tobacco factory at Keytesville, Missouri. I was then about ten years old, and although I had worked at Mr. Mean's place, I had done no steady work, because I was allowed many liberties, but at Judge Applegate's I was kept busy every minute from sunrise to sunset, without being allowed to speak a word to anyone. I was too young then to be kept in such close confinement. It was so prison-like to be compelled to sit during the entire year under a large bench or table filled with tobacco, and tie lugs all day long except during the thirty minutes allowed for breakfast and the same time allowed for dinner. I often fell asleep. I could not keep awake even by putting tobacco into my eyes. I was punished by the overseer, a Mr. Blankenship, every time he caught me napping, which was quite often during the first few months. But I soon became used to that kind of work and got along very well the balance of that year.

Orders had been sent to W. B. Bruce by Mr. Perkinson to bring his slaves back to Virginia, and about March, 1847, he started with us contrary to our will. But what could we do? Nothing at all. We finally got started by steamboat from Brunswick to St. Louis, Missouri, and thence to Cincinnati, Ohio. Right here I must tell a little incident that happened, which explains why we were not landed at Cincinnati, but taken to the Kentucky side of the river, where we remained until the steamboat finished her business there and crossed over and took us on board again. Deck passage on the steamer had been secured for us by W. B. Bruce, and there were on the same deck some poor white people Just before reaching Cincinnati, Ohio, some of these whites told my mother and other older ones, that when the boat landed at Cincinnati the abolitionists would come aboard and even against their will take them away. Of course our people did not know what the word abolitionist meant; they evidently thought it meant some wild beast or Negro-trader, for they feared both and were greatly frightened—so much so that they went to W. B. Bruce and informed him of what they had been told. He was greatly excited and went to the captain of the boat. I am unable to state what passed between them, but my mother says he paid the captain a sum of money to have us landed on the Kentucky side of the river. At any rate I know we were put ashore opposite Cincinnati, and remained there until the streamer transacted its business at Cincinnati and then crossed over and picked us up. The story told us by the white deck passengers had a great deal of truth in it. I have since learned that a slave could not remain a slave one minute after touching the free soil of that state, and that its jurisdiction extended to low water mark of the Ohio River. Slaves in transit had been taken from steamers and given their freedom in just such cases as the one named above. A case of this kind had been taken upon appeal to the Supreme Court of the state of Ohio, and a decision handed down in favor of the freedom of the slave. The ignorance of these women caused me to work as a slave for seventeen years afterwards

CHAPTER II.

Early in the spring of 1847, we reached the Perkinson farm in Virginia, where we found our master,
whom we had not seen for nearly three years, and his
son Willie, as he was then called, with hired slaves
cultivating the old farm. My older brothers, James
and Calvin, were at once hired to Mr. Hawkins, a
brickmaker, at Farmville, Prince Edward County,
Virginia.

In as much as it was not the custom in that state
to put slaves at work in the field before they had
reached thirteen years of age, I, being less, was
allowed to eat play and grow, and I think the happiest
doys of my boyhood were spent here There were
seven or eight boys about my age belonging to Mrs
Perkinson, living less than a mile distan' on adjoining
farms, who also enjoyed the same privileges, and there
were four or five hounds which we could take out rab-
bit hunting when we wished to do so It was grand
sport to see five or six hounds in line on a trail and to
hear the sweet music of these trained fox hounds.
To us, at least, it was sweet music. We roamed over
the neighboring lands hunting and often catching rabbits, which we brought home During the fishing season we often went angling in the creeks that meand-
ered through these lands to the millpond which
furnished the water for the mill near by, which was
run by Uncle Radford, an old trustworthy slave belonging t> Mrs. Prudence Perkinson. He was the lone

miller, and ground wheat and corn for the entire neighborhood.

There were several orchards of very fine fruit on these farms. We were allowed to enjoy the apples, peaches, cherries and plums, to our heart's content. Besides, there were large quantities of wild berries and nuts, especially chinquapins. When we had nothing else to do in the way of enjoyment we played the game of " shinney "—a game that gave great pleasure to us all. I was playmate and guardian for Willie Perkinson, and in addition to this I had a standing duty to perform, which was to drive up three cows every afternoon. At this time Willie was old enough to attend the school which was about two miles away, and I had to go with him in the forenoon and return for him in the afternoon. He usually went with me after the cows.

I had been taught the alphabet while in Missouri and could spell " baker," " lady," " shady," and such words of two syllables, and Willie took great pride in teaching me his lessons of each day from his books, as I had none and my mother had no money to buy any for me. This continued for about a year before the boy's aunt, Mrs. Prudence Perkinson, who had cared for Willie while we were in Missouri, found it out, and I assure you, dear reader, she raised a great row with our master about it. She insisted that it was a crime to teach a Negro to read, and that it would spoil him, but our owner seemed not to care anything about it and did nothing to stop it, for afterward I frequently had him correct my spelling. In after years I learned that he was glad that his Negroes could read, especially the Bible, but he was opposed to their being taught writing.

But my good time ended when I was put to the plow in the Spring of 1848. The land was hilly and rocky. I, being of light weight, could not hold the plow steadily in the ground, however hard I tried. My master was my trainer and slapped my jaws several times for that which I could not prevent. I knew then as well as I know now, that this was unjust punishment. But after the breaking season and planting the crop of corn and tobacco was over, I was given a lighter single horse plow and enjoyed the change and the work. Compared with some of his neighbors, our master was not a hard man on his slaves, because we enjoyed many privileges that other slaves did not have. Some slave owners did not feed well, causing their slaves to steal chickens, hogs and sheep from them or from other owners. Bacon and bread with an occassional meal of beef was the feed through the entire year ; but our master gave us all we could eat, together with such vegetables as were raised on the farm. My mother was the cook for the families, white and black, and of course I fared well as to food

Willie Perkinson had become as one of us and regarded my mother as his mother. He played with the colored boys from the time he got home from school till bedtime, and again in the morning till time to go to school, and every Saturday and Sunday. Having learned to spell I kept it up, and took lessons from Willie as often as I could. My younger brother, B. K. Bruce (now Ex-Senator) had succeeded me as playmate and guardian of Willie, and being also anxious to learn, soon caught up with me, and by Willie's aid went ahead of me and has held his place during all the years since.

Mrs. Prudence Perkinson and her son Lemuel, lived about one mile from our place, and they owned about fifty field hands, as they were called. They also had an overseer or negro-driver whose pay consisted of a certain percentage of the crop.

The larger the crop the larger his share would be, and having no money interest in the slaves he drove them night and day without mercy. This overseer was a mean and cruel man and would, if not checked by her, whip some one every day. Lemuel Perkinson, was a man who spent his time in pleasure seeking, such as fox-hunting, fishing, horse racing and other sports, and was away from home a great deal, so much so that he paid little attention to the management of the farm. It was left to the care of his mother and the overseer. Mrs Sarah Perkinson, wife of Lemuel Perkinson, was a dear good woman and was beloved by all her slaves as long as I knew her, and I am informed that she is living now and is still beloved by her ex-slaves Mrs. Prudence Perkinson would not allow her overseer to whip a grown slave without her consent, because I have known of cases where the overseer was about to whip a slave when he would break loose and run to his old mistress. If it was a bad case she would punish the slave by taking off her slipper and slapping his jaws with it. They were quite willing to take that rather than be punished by the overseer who would often have them take off the shirt to be whipped on their bare backs.

Mrs. Prudence Perkinson was a kind hearted woman, but when angry and under the excitement of

the moment would order a servant whipped, but before
the overseer could carry it out would change her mind.
I recall a case where her cook, Annica, had sauced her
and refused to stop talking when told to do so. She
sent for the overseer to come to the Great House to
whip her (Annica) He came and called her out ; she
refused to obey. He then pulled her outside and
struck her two licks with his whip, when her " old mistress " promptly stopped him and abused him, and
drove him out of the Great House yard for his brutality. She went to Annica, spoke kindly to her and
asked her if she was hurt.

I write of this as I saw it. I can recall only one or
two instances where our master whipped a grown person, but when he had it to do or felt that it should be
done, he did it well.

Our owner had one serious weakness which was
very objectionable to us, and one in which he was the
exception and not the rule of the master class. It was
this: He would associate with " poor white trash,"
would often invite them to dine with him, and the habit
remained with him during his entire life

There lived near our farm two poor white men,
better known at the South as "poor white trash,"
named John Flippen and Sam Hawkins. These men
were too lazy to do steady work and made their living
by doing chores for the rich and killing hawks and
crows at so much a piece, for the owner of the land on
which they were destroyed. These men would watch
us and report to our master everything they saw us do
that was a violation of rules. I recall one instance in
which I was whipped on account of a lie told by Sam
Hawkins. The facts in the case are as follows: I was

sent one Saturday afternoon to Major Price's place after some garden seed and was cautioned not to ride the mare hard, and I did not therefore take her out of a walk or a very slow trot as it was not to my interest to do otherwise, for the distance was but two miles and if I came back before sundown I would have to go into the field to work again. I got back about sundown, but had met Sam Hawkins on the road as I went, and he was at our house when I returned. He was invited to supper, and while at the table told my master that I had the mare in a gallop when he met me. Coffee was very costly at that time, too high for the " poor white trash; " none but the rich could afford it, and the only chance these poor whites had to get a cup of coffee was when so invited. It was always a Godsend to them, not only the good meal, but the honor of dining with the " BIG BUGS." Being illiterate their conversation could not exceed what they had seen and heard, and to please their masters, for such they were to these poor whites almost as much as to their slaves, they told everything they had seen the slaves do, and oftener more.

After supper that evening my master sent for me. When I came, he had a switch in his hand and proceeded to explain why he was going to whip me. I pleaded innocence and positively disputed the charge. At this he then became angry and whipped me. When he stopped he said it was not so much for the fast riding that he had punished me as it was for disputing a white man's word. Fool that I was then, for I would not have received any more whipping at that time, but knowing that I was not guilty I said so again and he immediately flogged me again. When he stopped he asked me in a loud tone of voice, " Will you have the impudence to dispute a white man's word again? " My answer was "No sir." That was the last whipping he ever gave me, and that on account of the lie told by a poor white man. But I lived not only to dispute the word of these poor whites in their presence, but in after years abused and threatened to punish them for tresspassing upon his lands.

Other ex-slaves can relate many such cases as the Hawkins' case and such instances, in my opinion, have been the cause of the intense hatred of slaves against the poor whites of the South, and I believe that from such troubles originates the term " poor white trash." In many ways this unfortunate class of Southern people had but a few more privileges than the slaves. True, they were free, could go where they pleased without a " pass," but they could not, with impunity, dispute the word of the rich in anything, and obeyed their masters as did the slaves. It has been stated by many writers, and I accept it as true, that the Emancipation Proclamation issued by President Lincoln, not only freed the slaves, but the poor whites of the South as well, for they occupied a condition nearly approaching that of slavery.

They were nominally free, but that freedom was greatly restricted on account of the prejudice against them as a class. They were often employed by the ruling class to do small jobs of work and while so engaged were not allowed, even to eat with them at the same table, neither could they in any way associate or intermarry with the upper classes. Of course this unfortunate class of people had a vote, but it was always cast just as the master class directed, and not as the voter desired, if he had a desire. I recall very clearly the fact, that at each County, State or National election the poor white people were hauled to the voting places in wagons belonging to the aristocratic class. They also furnished a prepared ballot for each man and woe unto that poor white man who failed to vote that ticket or come when sent for. Each one of the master class kept a strict lookout for every poor white man in his neighborhood and on election days sent his wagons and brought each one of these voters to the polls.

When the war of the Rebellion broke out this class of men constituted the rank and file of the Confederate army and rendered good service for their masters, who had only to speak a kind word to them when they would take the oath and obediently march to the front, officered by the aristocratic class. These poor people contributed their full share to the death roll of the Southern Army.

True to his low instinct, the poor white man is represented at the South as the enemy of the Colored people to-day, just as he was before the war, and is still as illiterate as he was then. He is not far enough up the scale to see the advantage of education, and will not send his children to school, nor allow the Colored child to go, if it is in his power to prevent it. It is this class who burn the school houses in the Southland to-day. The aristocracy and the Colored people of the South would get along splendidly, were it not for these poor whites, who are the leaders in all the disorders, lynchings and the like. The South will be the garden spot, the cradle of liberty, the haven of America, when the typical poor whites of that section shall have died off, removed, or become educated, and not till then.

CHAPTER III.

During the summer, in Virginia and other southern states, slaves when threatened or after punishment
would escape to the woods or some other hiding place.
They were then called runaways, or runaway Negroes,
and when not caught would stay away from home
until driven back by cold weather. Usually they would
go to some other part of the state, where they were not
so well known, and a few who had the moral courage
would make their way to the North, and thus gain their
freedom. But such cases were rare. Some, if captured and not wishing to go back to their masters,
would neither give their correct name nor that of their
owner; and in such cases, if the master had not seen
the notice of sale posted by the officers of the county
wherein they were captured, and which usually gave
the runaway's personal description, they were sold to
the highest bidders, and their masters lost them and the
county in which the capture was effected got the proceeds, less the expense of capture. A runaway often
chose that course in order to get out of the hands of a
hard master, thinking that he could not do worse in any
event, while he might fall into the hands of a better
master. Often they were bought by Negro traders
for the cotton fields of the South.

The white children had great fear of runaway
Negroes, so much so that their mothers would use the
term "runaway nigger" to scare their babies or to
quiet them. I was greatly afraid of them, too, because

I had heard so many horrible stories told of their brutality, but I have no personal recollections of any such case. I recall two instances where I had dealings with them. The first was as follows :—One of our cows had a calf two or three days old hid in the timber land, and I was sent to find it, and in doing so went into the woods where the underbrush was quite thick, and suddenly came upon a rough-looking, half clad black man. I was too close or too much frightened to run from him and stood speechless. He spoke pleasantly, telling me where I could find the calf, and stated that if I told the white people about him he would come back and kill me. He had a piece of roasted pork and " ashcake," and offered me some which I was afraid to refuse Of course I did not inform on him.

The other occasion was when I was sent to the mill about three miles distant with an ox-team and two or three bags of corn and wheat. I did not get away from the mill until near sundown, and when near home, while passing through a body of timber land, a black man stepped out in front of my oxen and stopped them. He looked vicious but said nothing. He got into the cart and cut one bag in half, taking about one bushel of meal, jumped out and let me go without further trouble. I told my master about this but nothing was done, it being Saturday night, and the only man near by who kept Negro hounds was Thomas Rudd, who would not go Negro hunting on Sunday.

These runaways lived upon stolen pigs and sheep, and the hardest thing for them to get was salt and bread. It was really dangerous for any person to betray one of these fellows, for when caught and carried home to their masters, they were usually whipped.

But they would run away again, come back, lie in wait for their betrayer, and punish him severely. Those who hired slaves belonging to estates, which under the law had to be hired out every year, often suffered in this respect, for it sometimes ha pened that the slaves would run away in the spring and remain away until Christmas, when they would report to the guardian of the estate, ready to be hired out for another year, while the employer was compelled to pay for the last year's service. I have known of several such cases.

I hope from what I have said about "runaways," that my readers will not form the opinion that all slave men who imagined themselves treated harshly ran away, or that they were all too lazy to work in the hot weather and took to the woods, or that all masters were so brutal that their slaves were compelled to run away to save life. There were masters of different dispositions and temperaments. Many owners treated their slaves so humanely that they never ran away, although they were sometimes punished; others really felt grieved for it to be known, that one of their slaves had been compelled to run away; others allowed the overseer to treat their slaves with such brutality that they were forced to run away, and when they did, the condition of those remaining was bettered, because the master's attention would be called to the fact, and he would limit the power of the overseer to punish at will; others never whipped grown slaves and would not allow any one else to do so. I recall an instance showing the viciousness of these runaway Negroes, which I think illustrates the point as to their hard character.

There was a slave named Bluford, belonging to a hemp raiser in Salene County, Missouri, who owned a large plantation, and owned a large number of slaves, and who had a poor white man employed as overseer. This overseer got angry at Bluford for some offence or neglect, and attempted to flog him, but instead got flogged himself and reported to the master the treatment he had received. The master sent for Bluford, and without making inquiry to ascertain the facts, proceeded to punish the slave, who in turn flogged his master and then ran away. The Missouri River is a very wide, rapid and dangerous stream, and runs between Howard and Salem counties, only a few miles from his master's plantation. By some means Bluford crossed it and hid himself in a wheat field on the other side of the river to wait till dark. He told me that he was hid in a corner of a fence, and the wheat being ripe was ready to be cut. Now what spirit lead the owner of the field to get over the fence right in that corner can never be known, but he did, and found Bluford, whom he grabbed in the collar, and refused to let go after being warned. Bluford was armed with a butcher's knife, and with it he cut the man across the abdomen, severing it to the backbone, causing death in a very short time. Hunting parties were immediately organized, who searched the surrounding country in vain for the murderer. I think this occurred in July, 1855. I had been acquainted with Bluford previous to that time.

Some time during the spring of 1865, I met Bluford on the street in Leavenworth, Kansas, after he had been to Kansas City, Missouri, to meet some relative. He gave me the facts in the case, and told me that he followed Grand River to its head water, which was in Iowa, then made his way to Des Moines, where he remained until the war, when he enlisted and served to the close of the war.

Bluford could read quite well when I knew him in 1855, and had paid attention to the maps and rivers of the state of Missouri.

Then there were different kinds of slaves, the lazy fellow, who would not work at all, unless forced to do so, and required to be watched, the good man, who patiently submitted to everything, and trusted in the Lord to save his soul; and then there was the one who would not yield to punishment of any kind, but would fight until overcome by numbers, and in most cases be severely whipped; he would then go to the woods or swamps, and was hard to capture, being usually armed with an axe, corn knife, or some dangerous weapon, as fire arms at that time were not obtainable. Then there was the unruly slave, whom no master particularly wanted for several reasons; first, he would not submit to any kind of corporal punishment; second, it was hard to determine which was the master or which the slave; third, he worked when he pleased to do so; fourth, no one would buy him, not even the Negro trader, because he could not take possession of him without his consent, and of course he could not get that. He could only be taken dead, and was worth too much money alive to be killed in order to conquer him. Often masters gathered a gang of friends, surrounded such fellows, and punished them severely, and at other times the slave would arm himself with an axe, or something dangerous, and threaten death to any one coming within his reach. They could not afford to shoot him on account of the money in him, and of course they left him. This class of slaves were usually industrious, but

very impudent.   There were thousands of that class,
who spent their lives in their master's service, doing
his work undisturbed, because the master understood
the slave.

I am reminded of a fight I once witnessed between
a slave and his master.   They were both recognized
bullies.   The master was a farmer, whose name I shall
call Mr. W., who lived about three miles from Brunswick, Missouri.   He had, by marriage I think, gained
possession of a slave named Armstead   Soon after
arriving 'at his new home his master and he had some
words; his master ordered him to "shut up," which he
refused to do.   The master struck him and he returned
the blow.   Then Mr. W. said, " Well, sir, if that is
your game I am your man, and I tell you right now, if
you lick me I'll take it as my share, and that will end
it, but if I lick you, then you are to stand and receive
twenty lashes."

They were out in an open field near the public
road, where there was nothing to interfere   I was on
a wagon in the road, about forty yards distant.   Then
commenced the prettiest fist and skull fight I ever witnessed, lasting, it seemed, a full half hour; both went
down several times; they clinched once or twice, and had
the field for a ring, and might have occupied more of it
than they did, but they confined themselves to about
one fourth of an acre.   Of course Armstead had my
sympathy throughout, because I wanted to see whether
Mr. W. would keep his word.   They were both bloody
and also muddy, but grit to the backbone.   Finally my
man went down and could not come to time, and cried
out, " Enough."   There was a creek near by, and they
both went to it to wash.   I left, but was informed that

the agreement was carried out, except that Mr. W. gave his whipped man but six light strokes over his vest. Could he have done less ? But I have been informed that these men got along well afterwards without fighting, and lived together as master and slave until the war.

I believe in that old saying, that blood will tell. It is found to be true in animals by actual tests, and if we will push our investigations a little further, we will find it true as to human beings.

Of course I do not wish to be understood as teaching the doctrine, that blood is to be divided into white blood and black blood, but on the contrary, I wish to be understood as meaning that it should be divided into inferior and superior, regardless of the color of the individual in whose veins it flows.

The fact of the presence in the South, especially, of the large number of the typical poor whites, held, as it were, in a degree of slavery, is a contradiction of the assertion, that white blood alone is superior.

If this class had superior blood in their veins, (which I deny) is there a sane man who will believe that they would have remained in the South, generations after generations, filling menial positions, with no perceptible degree of advancement ? I venture to say not. The truth is, that they had inferior blood; nothing more. To further explain what I mean relative to inferior and superior blood among slaves, I will state, that there were thousands of high-toned and high-spirited slaves, who had as much self-respect as their masters, and who were industrious, reliable and truthful, and could be depended upon by their masters in all cases.

These slaves knew their own helpless condition. They also knew that they had no rights under the laws of the land, and that they were, by those same laws, the chattels of their masters, and that they owed them their services during their natural lives, and that the masters alone could make their lives pleasant or miserable. But having superior blood in their veins, they did not give up in abject servility, but held up their heads and proceeded to do the next best thing under the circumstances, which was, to so live and act as to win the confidence of their masters, which could only be done by faithful service and an upright life.

Such slaves as these were always the reliables, and the ones whom the master trusted and seldom had occasion to even scold for neglect of duty. They spent their lives in their master's service, and reared up their children in the same service.

Such slaves were to be found wherever the institution of slavery existed, and when they were freed by the war, these traits which they had exhibited for generations to such good effect, were brought into greater activity, and have been largely instrumental in making the record of which we feel so proud to-day. Th s class of slaves not only looked after their own interests, but their master's as well, even i.1 his absence.

I recall a case in point. Some time during the fall of 1857, in company with a man belonging to Dr. Watts, who lived near Brunswick, Missouri, as we were passing his master's farm, one Sunday night, we heard cattle in the corn field destroying green corn. These cattle had pushed down the fence. I said to the man: "Let us drive them out and put up the fence."

His reply was, " It's Massa's corn and Massa's cattle,
and I don't care how much they destroy; he won't
thank me for driving them out, and I will not do it."

To the class of superior blooded slaves may be
added the fighting fellows, or those who knew when
they had discharged their duty, and by virtue of knowing this fact, would not submit to any kind of corporal
punishment at the hand of their master, and especially
his overseer.

Just as among the whites in the South there was
an inferior blooded class, so among the slaves there
was an inferior blooded class, one whose members
were almost entirely devoid of all the manly traits of
character, who were totally unreliable and were without self-respect enough to keep themselves clean.

They spent their lives much like beasts of burden.
They took no interest in their master's work or his
property, and went no further than forced by the lash,
and would not go without it.

They reared their children in the same way they
had come up, with no perceptible change for the better.
They had not the spirit nor the courage to resist punishment, and bore it submissively. From that class, I
believe, springs the worthless, the shiftless, the dishon-
est and the immoral among us to-day, casting unmer-
ited blame upon the honest, thrifty and intelligent
colored people, who strive to live right in the sight of
God and man.

Another view held by people who have given the
matter some thought, is this: there were masters of
quite different temperament and disposition. Some
had no humane feelings, and regarded their slaves
as brutes, and treated them as such, while there were

others, (a very large class) who were good men, and I might say, religious men, and who regarded slavery as wrong in principle, but as it was handed down to them, they took it, believing that they, by fair treatment, could improve the slave, morally a least, for it was generally believed, that if he was freed and returned to Africa, he would relapse into barbarism. This latter class of slave owners treated their slaves better by far, than the other class, and my belief and experience tend to show that they got better service from their slaves, and enjoyed more pleasure, being almost entirely freed from the disagreeable duty of inflicting corporal punishment. I have personal knowledge of cases where young slaves had violated important rules, and the master, instead of punishing them himself, would go to their parents, lay the case before them, and demand that they take action.

In cases where the master had confidence in his slaves, and they in turn had confidence in him, both got along agreeably.

So that the point I wish to make is, that with few exceptions, a good master made good slaves, intelligent, industrious and trustworthy, while on the other hand, a mean and cruel master made shiftless, careless, and indolent slaves, who, being used to the lash as a remedy for every offence, had no fears of it, and would not go without it. Some people assert that long-continued ill-treatment had taken all the spirit of manhood out of this class of slaves, and that it will take generations of schooling and contact with intelligent people to instill into them the spirit of manhood, self-respect, and correct ideas of morality

Admitting this to be true, I believe it is as much

the duty of the American white people to extend the necessary aid to these unfortunate people, as it is the duty of the better class among us, (the colored people), to do this work of uplifting them.

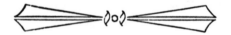

CHAPTER IV.

I recently visited my old home in Prince Edward County, Virginia, after an absence of forty-four years, and was greatly surprised at the changes which had taken place during that period. I had much trouble to find farms which I had knowledge of, because I remembered them only by the names they were called by in 1849. The owners of them had died or moved away and others had acquired the lands, changing the names of them, while other farms had been deserted and allowed to grow up in forests, so that with a few exceptions the country for miles in every direction was an unbroken forest of young trees.

Among the many notable changes which have taken place in this part of the State since 1849, are two or three to which my attention was particularly directed. The first is the entire change in the method of travel and transportation of freight and produce between Richmond, the western portion of the State and the Southern States.

The entire absence of the large number of six-horse teams, in charge of a colored driver and a water boy, that used to pass up and down the public road, which ran in front of our old home, and which extended from Richmond to the Blue Ridge Mountains, was quite noticeable, because that was the principal method by which freight and produce were carried.

That system of travel and transportation has been superseded by railroads, and goods are now delivered by the Richmond & Danville inside of three days after purchase, to any place on that railroad within two or three hundred miles. This railroad now runs parallel with the old public road from Richmond to the Blue Ridge Mountains and the South, and has entirely usurped the trade formerly monopolized by the old six-horse team system.

Very vividly do I recall the many six-horse teams which used to pass daily up and down that old road with their great loads of corn, wheat and tobacco, and return loaded with drygoods and groceries for the country merchants. I have seen as many as twenty of these teams pass our old home in one day. The teamsters, though slaves, were absolutely reliable and therefore, were intrusted with taking orders and produce from country storekeepers to the wholesale merchants in Richmond and on their return they would bring back the drygoods and groceries that had been ordered by the country dealers living along the road. Usually these wagoners went in squads of four or five and camped at the same camping grounds. The owners of these teams would come along about once a month paying and collecting bills.

These great wagons, covered with white canvas to protect the freight they bore, sometimes carrying from seven to ten thousand pounds and each drawn by six fine blooded horses, made to me at least, a grand and impressive picture, as the procession moved along the old road in front of our place. This picture was heightened by the picturesqueness of the colored driver in charge and his peculiar and characteristic dress. As he rode along on the sadle horse of the team he seemed conscious of the great responsibility resting upon his shoulders, and to the simple-minded colored people along the road he was simply an uncrowned king. When the wagons stopped at the camping grounds, located at regular intervals along the road, the colored people of the neighborhood flocked around to get a glimpse of this great man.

Although the freight was very valuable sometimes and often carried great distances, robbing or molesting these trains was something unheard of. They were perfectly secure while on the move or in camp, even in the most sparsely settled districts, because there were no robbers or gangs of thieves organized in those days to plunder passing teams   It is quite doutful whether the same would be true nowadays if a return to the old method of transportation was resorted to.

The country merchants in those days were content-ed and happy, I suppose, to be able to get their orders filled and goods delivered inside of from thirty to ninety days.

This great public highway, which was kept in such splendid condition in 1849 and prior thereto, and which had so many beautiful camping grounds where wood and water were convenient and not far apart, with lit-tle villages every ten or fifteen miles, where there were inns for travellers to rest and feed their horses has become a thing of the past along with that old system of travel and transportation. I have seen many men, called travelers in those days, pass over that old road going to, or from the South or West on horse-back, with large saddlebags strapped behind them armed with a horse pistol, which was about twenty inches long and as large as an old flint musket. Usually they carried a pair of these pistols hanging down in front of them, one on each side of the horses neck.

That was the usual way of travel in those days when persons wished to go a long distance, particularly to the West or South. Signs of this old road can yet be seen in places, but the road has been almost deserted, and has grown up in forest.

In front of our old place, and in fact from Miller's Store, a little village with a post-office, to Scofields, a similar place, a distance of ten miles, that old road was nearly on a straight line, was broad and almost level, and was the pride of that community ; but when I saw it in July, 1893, and attempted with a horse and buggy to pass over it for a distance of a few miles I found it impassable. From John Queensbury's Public Inn and Camping ground to our old home, a distance of three miles the old road has been entirely obliterated.

This road was kept in such a fine condition up to 1849 that many tobacco raisers used to put rollers around one or two hogs heads of tobocco, weighing about a thousand pounds each, then attach a pair of shafts and with a single horse draw them to Richmond, a distance of sixty miles.

I readily recall many different kinds of travel and trade which once thrived on this public highway. Richmond at that date being a great pork market and the most convenient one for the pork raisers of West Virginia and the Eastern portion of Kentucky, and this old public highway being the most direct route for travel from the West to Richmond, these hog raisers, in order to reach a market for their hogs, were compelled to drive them on foot over the road a distance of over two hundred miles. I have seen as many as three hundred hogs in one drove pass our old home in one day going towards Richmond. Usually these hog drivers brought along several wagon loads of corn to feed their hogs while en route. They could and did travel from ten to twelve miles a day, and from early fall to spring each year many thousand hogs were driven into Richmond over this public highway.

Besides supplying Richmond with pork, which in turn, furnished other places, especially in the South, these hog raisers sold hogs to planters on the road, who had failed to raise enough pork for home consumption. Pork was the principal meat diet at that time for both white and black, there being few sheep or beef cattle killed for table use, and then always for the table of the master classes.

To advise a farmer now living in West Virginia or Eastern Kentucky, who owns a hundred head of marketable hogs, to drive them two hundred miles to market, as his father had done, would be considered by him very foolish advice. But such was the only way of transportation of that kind of product prior to the year 1849, of which the writer has personal recollections.

These cases mentioned show clearly what railroads have done, not only for Virginia, Kentucky, and Tennessee, but the whole country and especially the Southern portion of it.

Richmond was also the principal slave market and this public highway the most direct route to the Southern cotton fields, especially those of Mississippi, Alabama, Louisiana, Arkansas, and Tennessee, and Negro traders passed over it many times each year with gangs of slaves bought at the public auction block in Richmond. I have seen many gangs of slaves driven over this old road. Usually, the slave men were hand-cuffed together with long chains between them extending the whole length of the gang, which contained as many as forty, sometimes, or twenty on each side of the chain marching in line. The women and small boys were allowed to walk unchained in the line while the children and the lame and those who were sick rode in wagons. The entire caravan would be under the charge of the owner and a guard of four or five poor white men armed each with a rawhide whip, with which to urge the gang along and to keep them in line or at least in the road.

It was not the custom, neither was it to the owner's interest, to treat these slaves brutally, for, like mules brought up to be carried to a better market, or where larger prices prevailed, it was absolutely necessary that they should not show any signs of ill-treatment; and I cannot recall ever having seen the punishment of one of them. Of course these Negro traders could not allow grown men to march in line unchained, particularly those who did not want to go, because they might become unmanagable, run away, and escape capture, thus causing the loss of the price paid for them, or at least give considerable trouble. As a general rule, many of these slave men were sold in the first place on account of insubordination—had resisted their masters, or had beaten their overseers, and such slaves were considered by their owners dangerous fellows on the farm with others, especially young men who might follow such examples. Then again many slaves were sold because they had committed murder or some other crime not deserving the death penalty, and there were no penitentiaries for slaves.

These and many other recollections of my early life crowded upon me as I looked upon the old familiar scenes. The absence of familiar faces was no less remarkable than the changes in lands and improvements, for I found only one man I had seen before. There were two others whom I knew in that vicinity and who had never left it, but I failed to find them at their homes. I visited the home of Mrs. Sarah Perkinson, widow of Lemuel Perkinson, mentioned in a previous chapter, but did not see her, as she had left a few days prior on a visit to relatives in North Carolina. I was really sorry I did not see her, for I could have obtained much valuable information from her, as she had remained in that community ever since the year 1849, and could have given me an interesting history of past events. She still owns the old Perkinson farm consisting of about two thousand acres. The old frame mansion which was built before 1841 was still there and in a fair state of preservation, and without any apparent change since I last saw it forty-four years ago. I found old man, Major Perkinson, one of Mrs. Perkinson's former slaves, occupying the Great House and tilling the land. There were about fifty acres under cultivation ; the balance had grown wild. The old Major who is now ninety years of age and quite active, remembered me very well and proceeded to treat me like a southern gentleman of the old school would have done. I next visited our old home which was one mile away. Here I found the great house, also a frame building, built in the summer of 1842, in a good state of preservation, and as I went through every room I am sure that there had been but little change in its structure. I also visited the spot where my

mother's cabin stood, and then how forcibly those lines
of the poet touched my mind, " Childhood days now
pass before me, forms and scenes of long ago," etc.
The quarters for the colored people had disappeared
here as well as those at Mrs. Perkinson's place. This
place is now owned by a Yankee lady in New York,
and of the six hundred acres under fence when we left
it in 1849, only four acres are now in use, the balance
having grown up in forest.

I visited several places of interest, and among
them was Green Bay, about two miles north of our old
home. Here I met Mr. Thomas Rowlett, the station
agent, and one, Mr. Scott, and a merchant named
Richardson, whose father I remembered. All three of
these men are direct descendants of the " Blue Bloods,"
and I found them still defending the right. I was
greatly impressed by a remark made by Mr Richardson; he said, " We are now, and will be for the next
twenty years, suffering from the curse of slavery; it
cursed the slave, it cursed his master, it cursed the
land." He then called attention to the thousands of
acres gone wild, too poor to produce anything, and the
owners were unable to bring them to a rentable condition, and the colored people could not make a living on
them and of course, left the country in search of work.
He said one could buy land anywhere in that community for three dollars per acre. Of course it will cost at
least ten dollars more to bring it up to a fair state of
cultivation. When I saw these fine lands in 1849,
tilled by slave labor, and kept in the very highest state
of cultivation, and on which splendid crops of tobacco,
corn and wheat were raised, I could not have realized
that in the space of forty-four years these same lands

would be a wilderness, the owners scattered, and even the former slaves gone. But so it is, and the names of the people who owned them forgotten. The only men I found who had remained and retained not only the old master's name, but the farm as well, were the Scotts, consisting of the father, two sons, Charles and Thomas, and a daughter, Mrs. Lefere. They had acquired the old homesteads of their old masters in each case and occupied the great house built of brick over sixty years ago, and still in good condition. These farms were adjoining each other and located on the Pike Road leading to Farmville, and near Sandy River Church. I remembered these farms and the Scotts very well, and also the church where my master used to go to worship quite often, and allowed his slaves to go occasionally on Saturday afternoon. Why I recall this so vividly is, because Sandy River was a clear deep stream with an abundance of fish, and while the older ones attended divine service I went fishing.

The Scotts, Col. Scott, Charles and Thomas A. Scott, brothers, were considered the most aristocratic people in that community, and owned quite a large number of slaves and treated them humanely, a fact which the father of the Scotts now owning the lands will testify to. Old masters are dead, and their children, having sold the old farms and scattered, their former slaves now own these estates and are industrious and thrifty fa mers. They had the best crops I saw in that country, with good stock in splendid condition I found the wife of Thomas Scott and Mrs. Lefere splendid houskeepers and entertained as none but Virginia ladies can. Each had one or more grown daughters, well educated, refined, and very pretty girls. I confess my surprise at finding such intelligent and fashionably dressed girls in that community.

CHAPTER V.

It is encouraging to note the advancement made upon the stronghold of ignorance, superstition and voodooism by the Colored people, since their emancipation from the bonds of slavery, and especially is this so to those who remember the time when a large majority of them believed strongly in all kinds of superstition, voodooism, gophering, tricking and conjuring.

I readily recall many instances wherein they were fleeced out of their little valuables or money by professional humbugs, known as conjurors, who succeeded in duping their fellow-slaves so successfully, and to such an extent, that they believed and feared them almost beyond their masters. I have known of cases where these conjurors held whole neighborhoods, as it were, in such mortal fear, that they could do unto the Colored people anything they desired, without the least fear of them telling their masters. These conjurors made all kinds of boasts and threats, as to what they could and would do to anyone who dared to interfere with them, or even dispute their word, or question their ability to carry out what they claimed to be able to do.

These conjurors claimed to be able to do almost anything in the line of impossibilities, even to taking life by the winking of their eye, to make a master be kind to a slave, to prevent him from selling one, even if he desired to do so, to make a girl love a man, whether she desired him or not, to make a man love and even marry a woman if she desired him.

For a stipulated sum paid them, they would give what was called " a hand or a jack," which they claimed would enable the holder to accomplish what he desired, and at the same time protect him from all harm, provided always, that the holder had faith and followed instructions.

These conjurors claimed to be able to bury a hand or a jack under the master's door step, which would prevent him from whipping a particular slave while it was there. Of course, if that particular slave got whipped, and so reported to the old conjuror, he would promptly claim one of three things, either that some-one had removed the jack, or that the fellow had failed to carry out instructions, or had no faith in the jack, and therefore was deserving of punishment.

These conjurors claimed to be able to put pain, or even permanent disability upon any one they desired, and could remove the trick put on by another conjuror, could cause live scorpions to appear under the skin of persons, and could take out those put there by other conjurors. They claimed that nearly every pain or ache was the result of conjuration, and the one sent for could take it off To show to what extent these people believed in voodooism, and could be fleeced, I will relate a story told me by Ike Cabel, of Brunswick, Mo. He said he was out with a surveying party about the year 1852, and camped near a large plantation in Louisiana. He gave it out among the slaves that he was a conjuror, and soon thereafter his camp was besieged every night by slaves with all kinds of aches and pains, which he cured with red clay, oak leaves and salt boiled, and collected fifty cents from each. A man came one night claiming that he had a scorpion in his

leg, and that he felt it running up and down the leg.
He told the man to come the next night, which he did.
The next day he wanted a live scorpion, and being
afraid of it himself, he got two young white men of the
party to catch one for him, promising them one-half he
was to receive for the job, and of course, let them into
the secret. They captured a scorpion, wrapped it up
carefully in brown paper, so that it could not escape or
bite, and delivered it to Ike.

After rubbing the man's leg for a while with his
other trick medicine with one hand, carefully holding
his little animal in the other, and when ready for the
final act, he looked heavenward, and in a loud voice
commanded the scorpion to come out of the man's leg.
Then in a few seconds he informed his dupe that the
animal had come, and at the same time, and by a
quick motion, freed the scorpion and brushed it from
the leg to the floor, when the freed scorpion attempted
to escape, and was killed and carried away by the patient after paying the three dollars

Now it would have been a hard job to convince
that poor, innocent, unsuspecting man, that he did not
have a live scorpion taken from his leg. His imagina-
tion was cured, and he was satisfied, and spread the
news far and wide of his wonderful cure.

It is claimed that the way scorpions and other
little poisonous animals or insects are gotten into the
body is through whiskey. That the little scorpion is
killed and laid out to dry, and when thoroughly dried
is beaten into dust, and the dust put into a bottle of
whiskey, and in a short time after being drank will
reproduce itself, whatever it is, under the skin of the
drinker. At any rate, I remember that conjurors were

never asked for a drink of whiskey, and people were always afraid to take a drink from some men's bottle until the owner had drank first, " to take the poison off."

These conjurors practiced with different kinds of roots, seeds, barks, insects, and other strange ingredients, but polk root and green planten were among their principal remedies to take off a trick or a pain. Of course they had some queer ways of mixing things to make it appear mysterious A poultice made of polk root is said to be a good remedy for rheumatism, and these conjurors probably knew that, and put in the poultice a few harmless things to make it appear strange, and if the rheumatic pain was removed, they would claim that they had taken off a trick put there by some conjuror. Of course different conjurors have different jacks and different " hands," but the two I saw were composed of hog-bristles, old horse shoe nails, a little red clay, salt, red pepper, red oak leaves, soaked in vinegar, then wrapped in a roll about three inches long and one inch thick, and tied with a yarn string very tightly. There is a peculiar lingo to accompany the " jack," and it varies according to requirements.

To show how thoroughly these people believed in conjurors, and to what extent they could be imposed upon by them, I will relate one more instance, which was told me by an old lady whose word I cannot doubt, and whom I have known for these many years, but to honor and cheer. She said that she belonged to one of two brothers living on adjoining farms in Amelia County, Va , prior to the year 1830, and that one of them was a bachelor and the other a widower, and that they loved each other dearly. That they owned about thirty slaves each, and that one of them decided to break up and take his slaves to Alabama, and made all arrangements to do so. When the day came to start, he gave the order to load the wagons and hitch up the horses, which was done, and that they remained standing, as did the slaves, until late in the afternoon, when the master came to the front door and gave orders to unload and unhitch the teams, and for the slaves to go to his brother's field to work. On the next day he left on horseback in company with another man bound for Alabama.

She said that many of his slaves did not want to go, and hearing of a great conjuror living ten miles away, made up a purse and sent for him. He came the night previous to the time set for starting to Alabama. My informant says, that he told them upon his arrival, that they had waited too long in sending for him, that if th y had sent for him earlier he could have stopped all, but now he could only stop the slaves from going, and even that would depend on whether the master walked over a "hand," which he was going to put under the front door steps. She says the old conjuror went to the front door steps of the great house about twelve o'clock that night, dug a small hole under the ground step, took from his pocket a little ball, talked to it a while in a whisper, then kissed it and put it in the hole, and covered it carefully and came away. That the slaves, she among them, watched the old master next morning, until they saw him come down the steps and walk around a while, then go back over this particular step. That they were then satisfied that the old master could not take them anywhere, and he did not.

I was never able to convince my dear old lady friend that all conjurors were humbugs, and this one was among them, and that it was purely a matter of chance so far as he was concerned. I do not want it understood that these conjurors were believed in by all Colored people, for there were a large number of intelligent ones, who paid no attention to conjurors, even defied them, told them that they were humbugs and liars. These conjurors were a shrewd set of fellows, and on that account alone were enabled to fool the less informed. They were industrious, and hard working, and faithful servants, and of course received no punishment, and were keen enough to point to this fact as evidence of the power of their jack in keeping their master under control, when, as a matter of fact, it was their faithful service alone that protected them from the lash.

There have been cases where Colored people took sick from some cause, and imagined themselves tricked or poisoned by some one, and the white doctor, unable to do them any good, gave up the case, and the patients, believing themselves poisoned and therefore incurable, have died, when they might have been saved, if the white doctor had only thought for a moment, and instead of giving up the case, announced himself a conjuror, and proceeded to doctor his patient's mind.

Superstition in some form has always existed, especially among illiterate people, regardless of color, and the more illiterate the greater the amount of superstition, and as a case of strong evidence of this, I point to the " spirit dance " by the Indians of the far West, where the excitement created by it has been so great, that an uprising was only kept down by the vigilance

of the regular army. While conjuring, tricking and
gophering, and the like, were believed in by the slaves,
and spirit dances and other forms of superstition were
practiced by the Indians, the American white people
believed as strongly in another form of superstition
called " witch craft," that they burnt innocent men and
women at the stake

In order to show that education and intelligence
are the great powers which have been the means of
dispelling the gloom of superstition and voodooism
among the Colored people especially, I will state that
the Colored people of Missouri, particularly those of
Chariton, Howard, Carroll and Randolph counties,
were above the ordinary slaves in the more extreme
Southern states in intelligence and education, and did
not believe in voodooism or conjuration nearly as much
as those in old Virginia, and when one was brought to
Missouri who claimed to be able to exercise those mir-
aculous powers, he was immediately laughed at and
openly defied by all excepting a few of the more illiterate. I recall one instance where a man named
Magruder, who owned about forty slaves, which he
brought to Brunswick, Missouri, from Virginia, and
bought land near the town and settled thereon. Among
his slaves was an old, whiteheaded, crippled man,
known as a conjuror. He claimed to be able to do
many mysterious and impossible things, and among
those who belonged to his master he was believed and
feared, but the Colored people in that vicinity laughed
at him, defied his threats, and denounced him as an
old humbug, for in truth such he was, and when those
who believed in him saw him defied and denounced,
and his inability to carry out his threats, they took

courage and denounced him too. When he saw his
business assailed and himself defied, with no more opportunity to gull the people, he gave it out that his
favorite plants and roots did not grow or could not be
found in that country, and that alone was the reason
why he could not practice his profession. The truth of
the matter was, that the Colored people in that state
were more intelligent than those from whence he
came, and therefore could not be easily humbugged.

CHAPTER VI.

After having traveled over the rich lands of the Western Country, where fine crops were raised without much effort, and especially without any fertilizer, our master could not be content to remain in the poor, hilly, rocky state of Virginia, and determined to go to Mississippi, where his sister, Mrs. Susan Green then lived So, about October, 1849, having sold the old farm he started with his slaves.

On this occasion there was a separation of man and wife. Eight or ten months previously, my sister Eliza had been married to a man named Tom, belonging to Nathan Fulks, who claimed inability to buy my sister, and her owner said he did not have the cash to spare to buy Tom, but offered to take him along and pay hire for him, which his master refused, and thus they were separated forever. She married again after six or seven years, but I never heard of Tom afterward.

While en route to Mississippi, Uncle Walt, before mentioned, was taken sick with some kind of a fever and had to be left for better care and treatment near the line of Virginia and Tennessee. His wife, Aunt Martha, did not want to be separated from him and was left, too. I have been informed recently that they were sold to the man with whom they were left. I remember when we lived in adjoining cabins that they were very quarrel ome people, and did not want their son Isaac to play with me, because, they said, I was a

" yarler nigger." I may have been a bad boy at that time and am not now prepared to say that I was not, but they used to treat me meanly in every possible way, and I often sauced them and ran when they got after me. I remember that I was wicked enough to be glad when they were left or sold, because they, particularly Aunt Martha, were always trying to raise trouble about something.

With one exception our master then owned only my mother and her children. By the first of December, 1849, we had reached the Greene plantation, located about fifteen miles from Holly Springs, Mississippi, which was a very large one and tilled by about three hundred slaves in charge of a very mean overseer.

The day after our arrival at this place, those old enough to pick cotton were sent to the field, and this was my first experience in cotton-picking We were called up by the overseer by means of a horn, ate breakfast and were in the field by daylight, sometimes, before it was light enough to see the cotton balls, and kept steadily at work till noon, when dinner was brought to us on large trays and the order given by the overseer to eat. We sat down right there, and as soon as the last mouthful was swallowed the order was given to go to work. We were given good, wholesome food and plenty of it, only the time was so short in which to eat it. From noon until dark we were driven by the overseer who carried a long whip called a blacksnake.

At dark, the females were allowed to go to their quarters, but the men and boys were divided into squads of five; each had a bale of cotton to turn out. Gins run by mules had been going all day, making lint cotton which had to be put in bales, and each bale had to stand under the press about twenty minutes, so that the last squad seldom got through earlier than nine o'clock; and this went on each day except Sunday.

Mr. Greene ran a large cooking establishment, so that when the work of the day was over supper was ready for all, and the horn was blown for breakfast an hour before daylight.

We remained here until January 1, 1850, when we were hired to Thomas Greene, a son of Mr. Greene, living about eight miles away. We got along without any punishment, while at old man Greene's plantation, but I saw others whipped. It has occurred to me since that our owner had something to do with this, for he was opposed to brutal treatment generally. He had hired us out for a year, but in March of that year he had become so dissatisfied with that country that he determined to leave it and go back to Missouri.

Slave owners, even Mississippians, were not all brutal. This was especially true of young Thomas Greene and his wife who were very good people. There was also a man named Cox, near by, who owned about four hundred slaves whom he treated very well. He gave them good quarters and built a church on his place and hired a white preacher to preach the gospel to them every Sunday, and compelled each slave to attend. He gave each man the use of an acre of land, and every Saturday afternoon to cultivate it One acre, well cultivated, would yield a bale of cotton which Mr. Cox would sell for them and buy whatever little things they might want, especially such as were not furnished by him. Usually this would be nice Sunday clothes, shoes, hats and Sunday wear for the women. I wish to state that Mr. Cox gave a half day every Saturday to

all of his slaves, and I state this from personal knowledge, having visited the Cox plantation many times and
played with the boys and girls thereon

There was also a large plantation south of the
Greene place, but the owner's name I cannot recall.
He owned a large number of slaves and I was told was
kind to them, but I remember that he allowed no visitors on his place, neither did he allow any of his slaves
to get outside of his fence at any time. He had some
very pretty girls about my age, and we met and talked
with the fence between us, on Sunday afternoon.

A near neighbor's cattle used to break into the
field and destroy corn and other grain on Green's plantation and I had to drive them out, and in doing so
threw a brick which broke the leg of one of them The
owner of it came over very soon and wanted to whip
me for doing it, and I supposed would have done so, as
he was a very large man, but Mr. Greene came to my
rescue, ordered him off the place and told him, " If you
whip the boy, I will whip you." He left, threatening to
whip me the first time he caught me off Mr. Greene's
land. I never went on this neighbor's land after that.

Having hired us out for a year, our master could
not rightfully claim us until the end of the time speci-
fied in the contract, unless he would give the time we
had served from January to March free, which he
agreed to do, and once more we were in his possession.
I am unable to express the joy we felt when he
informed us of his intention to take us back to Mis
souri. That was a great blessing to us, and the older
ones thanked the Lord for this deliverance. He came
to our quarters one Sunday afternoon and gave us this
very welcome news, and I remember that we were so

overjoyed that we could not sleep that night. He got
started about April 1, 1850. Having sold his teams
when we reached Mississippi, our owner had to hire
Mr. Greene's team to' haul us to Memphis, Tennessee,
where we took steamer bound for St. Louis, and thence
to Brunswick, Missouri. The trip was a pleasant one
and made in less than ten days.

There was much rejoicing when we were landed
at Brunswick, and were met at the levee by W. B.
Bruce, with a conveyance to take us out to his plantation, were we met old acquaintances, including my
brother and sister, who also belonged to him. We
were once more in the *state we loved and intent on
remaining whether our master liked it or not*, for he
had brought us where it was not so easy to take slaves
about without their consent, and besides some had
become men.

I recall that one Sunday, about two years afterwards, our master sent for the four men of us to meet
him at the home of W. B Bruce We did so and he
informed us that he had about made up his mind to
take us all to Texas. My older brothers, James and
Calvin, told him they would not go and I joined in. He
got angry and ordered us to " shut up," which we did.
He then told us to come back next Sunday, when he
would tell us what to depend on, which was done and
then, after seeing how bitterly his plans were opposed
by us he informed us that he would buy land and set-
tle in that country, which he did within two years.

After resting a few days upon our arrival at Mr.
Bruce's from Mississippi, we were all hired to one J. B.
Barrett, a tobacconist. My sisters were hired out as
house girls and mother as cook to a man named

Treadway, a school teacher, who was a mean man, not only to her, but to his wife as well. I don't think he ever struck my mother, but he abused her in every other way possible His wife was a good woman and treated mother humanely, but old Treadway was so mean that he would not allow any of mother's children to come to his kitchen to see her at any time, and in order to see her we used to wait until he was in bed, and then steal in. I don't think mother stayed there longer than that year.

The next two years she was hired to J. B. Barrett, who allowed his wife to manage the household affairs to suit herself, and as she was a very good woman and mother a good cook they got along splendidly, and Mrs. Barrett was well pleased with mother's style of cooking.

J. B. Barrett hired six of us for three years, and although he was a noisy kind of man, cursed a good deal and threatened to whip or have it done by his overseer, one Jesse Hare, he seldom punished anyone, especially those who were grown. I worked for him from June 1850, to January 1, 1854, and was whipped only once and that for fighting another fellow who had struck my younger brother, B. K. Bruce. This man, Charles Sanders, was a grown man at that time and I was an eighteen year old boy, yet I beat him so badly that he was disabled for work, at least two months thereafter. Knowing so well what would follow after this fight, I ran to the woods and made my way to my owner, about four miles distant But that did not save me for the overseer came after me, and after I had made my statement my owner's answer was, " You knew better than to fight and you will be whipped, and

I will do nothing to prevent it." I wanted him to pay
my fine and save me. He came to town with me, and
in the presence of J. B. Barrett and himself I was
whipped by old Jesse Hare, who did not like me and
took this opportunity to lay the lash on very hard, but
was promptly stopped by J. B Barrett and severely
reprimanded for his brutality.

This man Hare disliked me any way, because of
an old score, for previous to that he had attempted to
flog me and I resisted, and threatened to go to my
master. But I doubt very much, even now, whether
he would have protected me in such a case, for he was
so bitterly opposed to a slave's resisting or being saucy
to a white man.

After the factory closed in the fall of 1853, I was
hired out by J. B Barrett to a poor white man, named
David Hampton, and had not been with him more than
a month when one of his boys sauced me and I slapped him. He ran to his father who called me to him,
ordered me to take off my shirt, a thing neither my
master nor any other man had ordered me to do. Of
course I refused to obey and told him so in language
which he understood. He then threw a stick of cord-
wood at me which missed its mark, and I picked it up
and was about to throw it back, when he ran into the
house. This ended our fight. I would be ashamed of
myself, even now, had I allowed that poor white man
to whip me. But the fun came later. When supper
was called, the old man and his wife had eaten and left
the table, and the children, two girls and three small
boys and I ate together. Just as I finished and was
about to leave the table, the old lady came in behind
me with a hickory switch in hand. I could not afford

to resist her, neither could I get out until she had given me several severe blows. She left her marks on me, which I carried for several days, and I suppose she was satisfied; I know I was.

But after all, the Hamptons were very reasonable people and I was well pleased with them, and often visited them afterward. While they were poor people they were not the typical poor whites. Many of the parties mentioned are living and can take me to task if I misrepresent facts; but I have stated the truth in every particular, as I saw and experienced it.

There was a trait of character running through my mother's family, a desire to learn, and every member could read very well when the war broke out, and some could write. The older ones would teach the younger, and while mother had no education at all, she used to make the younger study the lessons given by the older sister or brother, and in that way they all learned to read. Another advantage we enjoyed was this: we were all hired to the same man and we worked and slept together in the same factory where, by hard work, we usually made some little money every week, which we could spend for whatever suited our fancy.

The men who hired slaves, and owners as well, had to feed and clothe them, and the slaves had no care as to those necessaries. Slavery in some portions of Missouri was not what it was in Virginia, or in the extreme South, because we could buy any book wanted if we had the money to pay for it, and masters seemed not to care about it, especially ours, but of course there were exceptions to the rule

But, returning to my life in the tobacco factory, I

must state that when we were hired out our owner notified the hirer that he did not whip any of his grown slaves, and would not allow it to be done by anyone else, and when the man who hired them found that he could not get along without punishing he should return them to him. That was the saving clause for us, but we did not take advantage of this to shirk or play; as proof of this I will state that there are men now living in Brunswick, who will bear testimony to the fact that the " Bruce hands," as we were called, brought the highest prices. Our master received from two hundred and fifty to three hundred dollars a year for each man or boy over seventeen years old, the hirer to feed and clothe us, etc

When the factory closed in September, 1854, I was hired to Charles Cabel, a farmer, recently from Louisiana, living about four miles from town and who owned twenty-five or thirty slaves, and was reported to be a very hard master I had been used to good fare, and that prepared and served clean and nice, but here the meals were served in such unclean vessels, while they may have been wholesome, I could not and would not eat them. W. B. Bruce lived only a mile away, and I went there to supper, stayed all night, took my breakfast and dinner with me to work.

In a few days Mrs. Susan Cabel found this out and sent for me; I explained and she said that her Negroes were so very dirty that she did not blame me, and from that date she sent my meals from her table, which came in nice clean dishes and in abundance. She was a good mistress as far as I knew.

Mr. Cabel had a very large number of lazy slaves and often inflicted punishment when, in my opinion, it might have been avoided. After I had been at his place about ten days he sent me with another fellow named Ike to split rails in a large body of timber north of his house. We had been at this work but a very short time, when I discovered Ike to be a lazy man. I had never been thrashed on account of laziness and did not want to chance it at that time, knowing the reputation of Mr. Cabel as a hard master. I had never split rails before and was put under Ike for training, and of course had to do as he directed. He was a great story-teller and would often stop to tell a story. I urged him to work but could not keep him at it over ten minutes at a time.

One day when we had cut off a log and I had commenced to split it, while Ike was sitting in the shade, I called on him to come and help me turn the log over, which he failed to do, and I went on working it alone. Mr. Cabel who had been watching near by and had heard all that was said came up, as if by magic, gun in hand, which he set by a stump, took out his knife, cut a hickory switch and ordered Ike to take off his shirt. Ike begged in vain, but he gave him thirty or more lashes on the bare back. During this exciting time I was scared almost to death, thinking my time would come next. I was tempted to break and run to my master, but knowing I had done my duty I concluded not to do so until I was called to take my share of this thrashing. I had determined to run if called and take chances on being shot, for I could not and would not stand such punishment as was given Ike. When he had finished whipping Ike he said, " Henry will work if you will let him; I have been listening to you for an hour." I can never express the relief those

words gave me, for I did not want to be forced to resist
and would not submit to any kind of corporal punishment, and was glad that I did not run while Ike was
being punished. I served out my term with Mr Cabel,
which ended December 25, 1854, without even being
scolded. Ike and I were separated after the above-
mentioned incident, fully half a mile, and I was given a
task which I performed easily every day. I shall speak
of Mr. Cabel again later on.

On January 1, 1855, with three younger brothers, I
was hired to Mr. Beasley, who owned a large tobacco
factory and worked about eighty hands, mostly hired. I
did not want to go there and told my master so in the
presence of Mr. Beasley, who asked the reasons why.
I told him that I had heard that he was a hard man to
please. My master remained silent during this conversation and finally Beasley and I came to terms, he
assuring me that if we worked for him as he had been
informed we did for Mr. Barrett, we would have no
trouble. After it was arranged my master took me
aside and severely scolded me for speaking so harshly
to Mr. Beasley. I took it easy for I never sauced him
at any time. But that was my opportunity to make
easy sailing that year with Beasley.

The overseer at this factory was named Tom
Black, who was really a much better man than old
Jesse Hare, and if one would do his work faithfully he
would have no trouble with Mr. Black He and I
became fast friends and I had an easy time, but I always
did my work well. Beasley gave an order that four
men were to come to his residence after the factory
closed, at sunset each day to cut or saw wood. When
my time came I refused to go. He was informed of the

fact and said he was going to have Tom Black whip me the next day, which was Saturday; in fact he told him in my presence to do it on Monday morning. But previous to this he called me up to know why I disobeyed his order. I told him that I was not hired for that purpose. Oh, but how he did cut up, yet he did not attempt to strike me.

Before going home to my master, which I certainly should have done, I thought it best to use a little strategy. During Sunday I had a talk with Mr. Black in which I told him my plans. He advised me not to go, and said that unless ordered again he would not attempt to whip me, and even then he would give me plenty of chance to run; but he said he would go and see Mr. Beasley that day. Now what passed between them I am unable to state, but when Mr. Black returned he said it was all right, and it was, for I was never molested after that, and Mr. Beasley revoked the order and had two men detailed to saw wood about four o'clock every evening. I had no more trouble that year with Beasley or his overseer.

I enjoyed life in the factories very much. We had good wholesome food and plenty of it, and when the factory closed at sunset we were free to go where we pleased until sunrise next day. I remember that the M. E. Church, South, allowed the colored people to meet in the basement of their church, and their minister preached to them every Sunday, commencing at three o'clock, P. M., and his text was not always from Luke xii. 47, or Titus ii. 9, but I have no recollection of hearing one preached from Ephesians vi. 9, where the duties of master to servant are explained. Some of the ministers were good men and preached reasonable sermons giving good advice, spiritually and morally, and were beloved by their colored congregations. I remember one whose name was W. G. Cooper, who was so well admired by his colored flock that they raised forty-five dollars and presented him a suit of clothes, when he went to conference, and sent a petition to have him returned to that charge.

Nearly every slave made some money which he could spend for fine clothes or such other things suited to his taste, so that when attending church I remember that the slaves were dressed almost as nicely as their owners, at any rate they looked as well as I have seen them on like occasions since they have been free.

We had some colored preachers, too, who held prayer meetings in their quarters and preached every Sunday afternoon in the white people's church, but there was always some leading white man present to take note of what the preacher said. If he used words deemed insubordinate or not in keeping with the pro-slavery idea, he was promptly stopped, there and then, and lectured for his mistake, and in some cases his license was recalled. Of course these licenses were granted by his master to preach during good behavior. Not three in ten of these preachers could read their texts or any other part of the Bible, but they stood in the pulpit, opened the Bible, gave out the song which did not always fit the tune, and delivered prayer with much force and in language that, while not the choicest, greatly impressed its hearers

There were a few colored men who could read the Bible, in and around Brunswick at that time, but none of them were preachers. The men who felt themselves called to preach had no education at all, but had a fair amount of brain, good memories, were fluent talkers, and considered pious and truthful. They could line a hymn from memory as clearly as their masters could from their books, and take a text and state were it was to be found.

I remember a story told on Uncle Tom Ewing, an old colored preacher, who was praying on one occassion, after the close of his sermon, in the church near Jacob Vennable's place, five miles from Brunswick. The old fellow got warmed up, and used the words, " Free indeed, free from death, free from hell, free from work, free from the white folks, free from everything." After the meeting closed, Jacob Vennable, who sat in front of the pulpit took Tom to task and threatened to have his license revoked if he ever used such language in public. Jacob Vennable was a slave holder and considered a fair master, so I was informed by Jesse, one of his slaves, and others who were supposed to know. I heard Uncle Tom preach and pray many times after the above-described occurrence, but never heard him use the words quoted above.

I remember when a question as to the purity of Christians (whether two clean sheets could soil each other) was being agitated among the colored people in the Bluff, as the hilly portion of the country, fives miles east of Brunswick, was then called It was argued pro and con with considerable warmth on both sides by the preachers and lay members. Considerable excitement was created thereby, and pending this the white men called a meeting and ordered some of the leading advocates of this new doctrine to appear before them, and they were then and there notified that if they did not stop that kind of talk, they, the white people, would whip every man who favored the clean sheet idea. That ended the new idea and I heard no more of it. I was then living on a farm in that neighborhood and know whereof I speak.

There is this to be said for the slaveholders in that part of the country, at least, that they believed in having their slave women live a virtuous life, and encouraged them in getting married, and did not under any circumstances allow plural marriages among them. Of course there would be occasionally a strange freak, a black mother with a very light-colored child, whose real father's name was never stated, but these cases were rare, the exception rather than the rule. When two lovers became engaged, the consent of the girl's parents, and that of both masters, if they belonged to different owners, had to be obtained. Then the girl's master would give them a wedding supper, and invite a few of his white friends, who would dine first, then the bridal party and their invited guests. The ceremony was usually performed by a colored preacher. After supper dancing commenced, which lasted until a late hour, when they would disperse. The master had built and furnished a cabin for the couple, and when the time came to retire, they were conducted to their cabin and left, after receiving many blessings.

I have stated in this chapter, that there were many masters who encouraged slave girls in their efforts to live virtuous lives, and in a former chapter, I stated that there were thousands of high-toned families, although held in slavery by the laws of the land, and who clearly understood their helpless condition, and yet, by reason of having superior blood in their veins, were enabled thereby to attain the very best conditions possible under the circumstances. These people were very sensitive as to their moral character and standing, and abhorred disgrace and dishonor. To prove this I will cite a case which occurred, and one of which I have personal knowledge.

There lived a slave owner named V. Harper about nine miles from Brunswick, Missouri, who owned quite a number of slaves. Among them was an old man, his wife, and several grown children, one of whom was a very good-looking girl, about nineteen years old This family were considered high-toned and greatly respected by others, even their owners, for their moral worth and character, and held themselves quite above the common slave.

The girl above mentioned was considered to be of clean character and quite a belle. It is not known who led her from the paths of rectitude, but when she became aware of the fact, that at no distant day, she, a single girl, would become a mother, and realized the dishonor and loss of character which would follow the exposure, she decided that death was preferable in her case to disgrace, walked two miles to reach the Missouri River, plunged herself into it, and was drowned. This occurred about the year 1858.

CHAPTER VII.

From 1857 to 1862 times had become rather hard on slaves in Chariton County, Missouri, and were very little better for the free Negroes, for while they were called free, they really had but few more privileges than the slave. They had to choose guardians to transact all their business, even to writing them a pass to go from one township to another in the same county. They could not own real estate in their own right, except through their guardian, neither could they sell their crop without his written consent. Of course, he made a charge for everything he did for them, which was quite a drain upon their resources. There were two or three families of free Negroes in that county, and some of them I often visited. In some cases slave owners did not allow their slaves to associate or in any way communicate with free Negroes, but our owner did not prohibit us in this respect, neither did W. B. Bruce.

Previous to 1840, an old man named Brown, and his wife, together with their slaves, came to Chariton County from the South. They had acquired seven hundred acres of land in that neighborhood, which were located about ten miles from Brunswick. They decided to set their slaves free and leave to them, by will, all their earthly possessions. In order to fit these freed people for the battle of life, they determined to educate them, and for this purpose started a school on the plantation, with themselves as teachers. All who were old enough were compelled to attend. I am unable to state exactly the date when this commenced, but remember that those old enough to attend it could read and write fairly well when I became acquainted with them in 1850. Unfortunately these people did not succeed well; they became poorer each year after the death of their master.

There were found many causes for this state of affairs. The property was left to them as a whole, and was only to be subdivided under certain conditions named in the will. All were not industrious, and the thrifty had to support the lazy. The agent claimed the right to sell the crop each year and divide the earnings equally among the several families.

By order of the Court the plantation was sold in 1855, and the proceeds divided equally among them, after which the families soon scattered, some going to Iowa, and others to Illinois. I have not heard from any of them since. The general opinion was that their guardian, P. T. Abel, got the cream of that estate, because when he arranged the sale of the plantation to Captain Withers, he retained five hundred dollars of the three thousand for his own professional service.

As already stated, there were three families of freed Colored people in that county, and they could only visit one another occasionally, because they lived about ten or fifteen miles apart ; to do so they had to secure a written permit from their guardian, for if one of them was caught on the public road without a pass, he was subject to arrest by any white man who chose to make it. Respecting these families of free Colored people, I wish to state that there was one exception, Davy Moore, or "Free Davy," as he was called, who

lived about five miles from Keytesville, the county seat
of Chariton county. He was a man of good character,
industrious habits, and greatly respected by the better
class of white people. On account of faithful and
efficient service, his old master, Colonel Moore, gave
him his freedom, also that of his wife and children, and
eighty acres of land   He was treated like a man; held
the respect not only of the Colored, but the white people as well, and enjoyed the same privileges as any
other man, excepting the right to vote. In his veins
flowed superior blood, and as has already been stated
in a former chapter, that blood will tell, regardless of
the color of the individual in whose veins it flows.

Singularly enough I had more real pleasure and
real freedom than these free people, for with my master's horse and a pass from him I could ride over the
county, in fact did whenever occasion demanded it, and
without molestation. If disturbed I had only to show
my pass, when I would be immediately released.

Two older brothers of mine, who were bricklayers
and stone masons, hired their time from their owner
and travelled, not only in the county where we lived,
but also in the adjoining counties of Carroll, Howard
and Randolph, in search of work, armed with a pass
good only in Chariton County. They had no trouble
even outside of that county, because they were known
as slaves. They made their own contracts, collected
their pay, and were not disturbed.

I recall but one instance where either of them had
any trouble. One of them had secured a job in Randolph County by underbidding a white man. Upon
finding he belonged to a man living in another county,
this white man had him arrested. He was carried to

Huntsville, the county seat, for trial. Fortunately there was a man there named Cass Wisdom, who knew our family, and who had him promptly released and became responsible for my brother's behavior while in that county. So that the only difference between the slave and the free Negro, as I saw it, was that the latter had no boss to make him work, or punish him if he did not; he could ride over the county every day if only provided with a pass from his guardian; he could spend his earnings as he pleased after paying his guardian's share They certainly did not have as much fun as I had, going to balls and parties given by slaves, where they were not allowed to come. But still the free fellows felt themselves better than the slave, because of the fact, I suppose, that they were called free, while in reality they were no more free than the slave, until the war set both classes free. So bitter was the feeling existing in Kansas in March, 1864, that those who became free by the war were called, in derision, by the freeborns, " contrabands."

An effort was made in Leavenworth, Kansas, in 1865 or 1866, to organize a combination or social circle, which allowed no contraband to be in it. The object of this organization, as I understood it, was to control everything in which Colored people had a voice, and it was to some extent successful, or at least for a while. During those years a steady stream of contrabands poured into Kansas, and soon constituted about ninety per cent. of the colored population. In a few years many had acquired little homes and standing, and had learned not only the object of the free class, but their own strength, and it was not long before they had relegated many of these would-be leaders to the

rear   Of course this brought about a conflicting and
unfortunate state of affairs.   The freeborns managed to
keep control of politics and especially the church and
other societies; they not only found, but created places
for one another   For a long time after the war, a contraband preacher, however competent he might be,
could not get a charge that would give him a decent
support.   All the fat places in the connection were
given to the other class.   If a contraband was sent to a
small charge, and worked it up so as to get a fair living
out of it, and so reported to the conference, by some
means he was replaced by one of the other set, and
sent further out.

I remember a worthy man named Jesse Mills, now
dead, who was a man of clean character, and had some
education, or at any rate could read and write ; he had
been preaching before the war, and was a slave.   For
nearly ten years that man did not get a decent charge,
and if he brought one up to the point where it supported him, he had to go in order to give place to some
fellow preacher from the North, out of a job.

There were others served equally as badly as Jesse
Mills, whose names I have not the space to mention,
save one, who I feel should not be overlooked.   Rev.
Moses White had been a preacher for several years
prior to the war, could read and write, in fact preached
quite an intelligent sermon, but not such an one as
would suit the conference; he therefore could not get
a charge.   He had been one of the men who organized
and built the Colored A. M E. Church at Leavenworth, prior to 1864; but he could not be or was not
assigned to any charge in that conference, and about
1867 or 1868, knowing or feeling that he had been

called to preach the gospel, he left the conference and organized a church on his own responsibility.

I write of these matters as I knew them, not being a member of any church at that time. In after years young men got in, such as W. A. Moore, an ex-slave, a man of clean character and of fine education, and greatly beloved by all who knew him; J. W. Wilson, who had been a slave and a brave soldier, and others of their class, self-educated men. They soon superseded those old fogies or leeches, if the term is admissible. So clearly and successfully has this been accomplished by the admission of young men, sons of ex-slaves, that to-day the term "contraband," or "freeborn," has been forgotten. But I have drifted away from my subject, "slavery, as I saw it on a plantation in Missouri," and with the permission of the reader, will return, taking up the line of recollections where I left off.

CHAPTER VIII.

Early in the Spring of 1856, our master had bought the Mann Plantation, located about seven miles east of Brunswick, and had made all arrangements to move to it, taking mother and four of her children, including myself. I did not want to go, but my desires in that respect were not considered, and I went without entering even a mild protest. Having lived in the city so long, I had lost all love for farm life. I had no knowledge of farming, especially that kind carried on in that part of the state, and personal experience taught me that my master possessed but little more than I did, because he ordered so many things done that were a loss of time and money. In his experimenting, for such it was, he would give an order one day, and change it the next, causing the loss of many days of labor. But it was my duty to obey him, right or wrong, and I did it right along.

After I had gained some practical knowledge, by experience, of the system of farming in that county, I ventured to suggest to him when I saw a better plan, or the uselessness of the order given. Of course he would not take the course I had suggested at the time, and in its entirety, but after thinking it over, he would change his orders as nearly to my plans as possible, without adopting them. But, oh, how I would catch it if he found flaws in them afterwards.

He worked the first year on that plantation almost as steadily as any of us, but that was his last year of work while he was my owner. He was a man who never talked much to his slaves at any time, as I have worked with him without a word being said, aside from my duty, between us many days, and I rather preferred it, because if he said anything, it would usually be scolding. I have a very clear recollection of the amount of scolding I got the first Spring on that farm, when laying off corn and tobacco rows. It was my first effort, and in nearly every row there would be one or more crooks, for which he would scold, then take my horse and plow, straighten the row, and give them back; pretty soon I would have it as crooked as before. The result of all this was that I soon learned to lay off a row nearly as straight as he could, and I will state that he could and did lay off the straightest ·row I had ever seen. He insisted that corn grew better in straight rows than in crooked ones, and I became convinced of the truth of his statements and took pride in having every row as straight as it laid off by line, and have been complimented on account of it.

At this plantation we had some neighbors whom I did not like, men who came from Kentucky and other southern states, and who tried to keep up the customs in vogue in those states of curtailing the liberties of their slaves, liberties which slaves in other parts of Missouri enjoyed; but even then the life of a slave in that part of Missouri was far better than in some of the older slave states.

Being a green hand at farming, I made many mistakes, which caused the boss to scold, but as that was all the punishment he inflicted, I soon became used to that, and went ahead doing the best I could. My boss really delighted in scolding; he could quarrel, make more noise, and do less whipping than any man in that county. He was not mean, in the sense that some of his neighbors were, and I have always believed that he tried to appear to his neighbors what he was not, a hard master. The reason why I entertained this belief is that in the presence of a neighbor he always scolded more, acted more crabbed, and was harder to please than when alone with us, for as soon as the neighbor left, we could get along with him very well. We were well fed, had such vegetables as were raised on the farm, and save biscuit and coffee, we had such food as was prepared for him.

Farming in Missouri consisted in raising tobacco, corn, wheat and stock, but tobacco was the principal product for sale. With five hands we usually raised about twenty thousand pounds, which at that time sold in Brunswick for about eight cents per pound. Each man was allowed one acre of ground to raise his own little crop, which, if well cultivated, would produce about nine hundred pounds of tobacco. We used his horse and plow, and worked our crop as well as we did his in the daytime, and when ready for market, he sold our crop with his, giving each one his share. This was our money, to be spent for whatever we wanted aside from that given by him. He gave two suits of summer and one of winter clothes, hats and boots, blankets and underwear. Our cash was spent for Sunday clothes, sugar, coffee and flour, for we would have biscuits at least once a week, and coffee every day.

The practice of allowing slaves ground to raise a little crop obtained generally among slave owners, but most of them had to work their crop of tobacco after sundown, and without plowing. The master got the benefit of this money after all, because the slave spent it for his own pleasure and comfort, which was a direct advantage to his master.

There were several slave owners around us at this farm, some were called mean and some considered fair, but the meanest man near us was a Yankee teacher, preacher and farmer, S. J. M. Bebee, who owned or hired four or five slaves, and treated them very meanly. This man came to that county from the East, and by teaching and preaching saved up money enough to buy a farm, and was considered by the Colored people meaner than the original slave-holders I lived on a farm within two miles of Mr. Bebee's farm, and had good opportunities to know the truth of what I state.

There lived near our home an old gentleman named Ashby, usually called "Father Ashby," who was a good man, much beloved by white and black, and who dropped dead in the pulpit at the close of one of his sermons. Previous to his death I used to visit his place, and sometimes we exchanged work. He owned three or four slaves and treated them kindly. Pending the campaign of 1856, when Fremont was the Republican nominee for President, I had a talk with "Father Ashby." He then said that he believed slavery to be wrong, but it was handed down to him from his father, and although he held and owned slaves, he had never bought or sold one, and had always treated them well.

I had learned to read, and could understand enough of the political situation at that date to be a "Fremont man," but a very silent one. I am safe in saying that Fremont did not receive one vote in Chariton County

at that election.   Certainly there was not an outspoken
Republican in the county.   Slave holders never talked
politics in the presence of slaves, but by some means
they learned the news, kept posted as to what was
going on, and expected to be set free if Fremont was
elected.   A Colored man who could read was a very
important fellow, for they would come miles and bring
stolen papers for him to read to them at night or on
Sunday, and I have known them to go to town and
buy them from Dr. Blue, an old slave-holder, and bring
them to some slave who could read.

Our owner did not like the farm he owned, and
early in 1857 sold it, and bought uncultivated land
adjoining his brother-in-law, W. B. Bruce.   Here I had
to open a place in the brush for a home, and for our
own quarters, assist in putting up buildings, make the
rails necessary to fence eighty acres of land, break it up
and put in a crop, all of which was accomplished in
one year.   I had got used then to farm life, and rather
enjoyed it.

This farm was only one-half a mile from W. B.
Bruce's, and the families were now practically together.
Our master and his son, Willie, spent a great deal of
their time at Bruce's, and so did the Colored families.

I was then a full fledged foreman with four
younger brothers, who constituted my force, but as a
matter of fact, I got more scolding than any one of
them, for the reason that I was held responsible for
everything, as our owner seldom went over any part of
the farm, and left me to manage it entirely, reporting
to him every morning.   I really had full control of the
place, but he did not want me to think so, and acted
rather queer quite often.   He had a habit of calling me

to his door every morning after breakfast, to report what was done the previous day, and what I thought should be done that day. I would state my opinion, and he would be certain to make light of it, get angry, tell me I had no sense, etc., make some suggestions, then cool down and tell me to go ahead and do just the work I had suggested. He, I believe, enjoyed that kind of acting, and I had got used to it and took it quietly, for that was the extent of my punishment.

We had but one neighbor who was called a hard master, Charles Cabel, for whom I had previously worked. Cabel had rather a lazy set of slaves, with one exception, a young man named Samuel Savage, and this, I suppose, made him appear meaner than he really was. His farm joined ours, and therefore I could hear and see much that was done. I am not an apologist for Mr. Cabel simply because he treated me nicely, not only when I was hired to him, but often afterwards on our farm. He saw what fine crops we raised every year, more and better tobacco, which sold for more money than his, while we worked but five hands, and he had ten or twelve.

There was no whipping on our place at any time, while on his some one was whipped nearly every week. Mr. Cabel used to come over on our land and talk with me quite often, and insisted that his Negroes made him appear mean, that if he had such Negroes as we were, he would never hit one. He said this to me many times; yet his slaves called him the meanest man in the county I am safe in stating, that I had more talk with Mr. Cabel during the five or six years we lived as neighbors, than with any slave owner during my service as a slave. Often he would come where I was at work and entertain me for an hour; he evidently enjoyed my company, and I confess a liking for him.

I recall an instance where he whipped four of his men within calling or hearing distance of me. I went to the timber to make some rails. Our timber land, which was four miles away, joined Mr. Cabel's, and he sent four of his men to make rails, and we all went on Monday. With the aid of a brother about sixteen years old, I had cut and split four hundred rails by two o'clock, or thereabouts, on Wednesday, not quite three days. Mr. Cabel came to me and asked when I commenced, and on being told, proceeded to count my rails, and when through, went over to where his men were. I don't think he found them at work; at any rate, in a short time, I heard the lash and the men begging for mercy. Pretty soon he came back to me, and said his men had made only two hundred and sixty rails, and then asked if I blamed him for punishing them. What could I say under the circumstances, knowing that there were four of them as against two of us, and one a mere boy?

My opinion is that Mr. Cabel as well as his slaves were to be blamed for the condition that existed on that farm, based upon the following reasons: The master who treated his slaves humanely had less trouble with them, got better service from them, and could depend upon their doing his work faithfully, even in his absence, having his interest in view always. Maltreated slaves and ill-treated beasts of burden are much alike; if trained to be punished, whether deservedly or not, they take no interest in their service, and go no further than the lash forces them, because they receive no encouragement even when they perform their duty well.

I recall a case in point, and as the parties mentioned are living I call upon them to set me right if I
misrepresent the facts in the case. My master bought
three yoke of oxen to break up this new land heretofore mentioned, much of which was covered with hazel
brush about four feet high, and to haul rails and fire-
wood from the timber land four miles away. I had the
sole management of this team, in fact had to break them
in. I took pride in that team, trained my oxen to obey
without the use of the whip, fed and watered them well
under all circumstances, and they looked sleek, fat and
cheerful, if I may use the term for an ox. I was the
master in this case and almost loved my oxen, and
believe they loved me. When I said "Go," they went,
regardless of the load, and the question was whether
the wagon would bear it up.

W. B. Bruce, before mentioned, owned three yoke
of oxen and a driver named Bob or Robert Bruce, who
had no love or mercy for his team, took no pride or
interest in his oxen, not even enough to feed and water
them regularly. He used a rawhide whip, and I have
seen him break their hides and bring out the blood
when using the lash. I have said he did not feed them
well, and the reasons why I say it are these: His
master, W. B. Bruce, always raised plenty of corn and
other kinds of stock feed and allowed his dumb crea-
tures enough, and there existed no sufficient reasons
why Bob's team should not look as fat and as sleek,
and draw as heavy a load as mine; but they did not,
and the reasons are very plain. I cared for mine, and
by so doing won their confidence and love and obedi-
ence, without the use of the lash, while Bob used the
lash in the place of kind treatment and kind words.

In 1857, the county had become pretty thickly settled with pro-slavery men from the South, mostly from Virginia and Kentucky, with a few Eastern men and Germans. Of course the men from the East, as soon as they landed, proclaimed themselves in favor of slavery and often hired slaves, and in such cases treated them meaner than the slave owner. They, it seemed, regarded the slave as a machine which required no rest, and they gave him none; they would drive the slave in all kinds of weather without mercy, so much so that slaves who belonged to estates or others who were for hire, would beg to be hired to some southern man, who had a knowledge of slave labor and the slave.

The Germans were quite different; they never hired slaves, and I can recall the name of only one who owned a slave. His name was Goss and he lived about six miles North of our place. He treated his slaves as he did his children; he owned four or five.

There was a lot of poor white trash scattered over that county, as there was in other southern states, and they answered the same purpose, as servants to their masters. But few of them could get a job as overseer, for the reason that there were but few large slave owners in that county; I mean that there were not a dozen men in the county owning over forty, and most of them owned less; they did their own over-seeing. But I must say that the poor whites, as a general thing, in that county at least, worked hard for a living, and I can mention several who, by dint of hard labor and economy, attained to a fair standing in their community.

After the landing at Brunswick, of the first install-ment of Germans, and as they obtained homes and money they sent for relatives and friends in Germany, so that there was a steady stream of German immigrants to that county each year up to 1864. But from 1853 to 1864, they had to submit to many indignities from ultra pro-slavery men. I have seen them kicked off the principal street without resistence by Col. Pugh Price, a brother, I think, of Gen. Sterling Price. But still they came, and soon some of them had opened business places such as cooper and shoe shops, cake and candy stands, and finally a brewery. It was wonderful to see how rapidly the people learned to drink lager beer made by a German, John Stroebe.

There was a large tract of land five or six miles below Brunswick, called Bowling Green, which lay quite low and was sometimes overflowed by the Missouri River. It was considered unhealthy in that localtity and on that account the land sold cheap. The Germans bought the greater part of it and formed quite a settlement. This land was known as the richest in the county and retains that reputation to-day, and is thickly settled and about as healthful as any other part of the county, is more valuable and is still owned by Germans whom we considered quite prosperous farmers.

There was a feeling created against these people about 1859 and 1860, caused by some suspicious pro-slavery men charging them with talking to slaves, and I cannot say they were not guilty They were opposed to slavery and when they had an opportunity to tell a slave so, without his master's knowledge, they often did it, especially if they had confidence in the slave. Slaves never betrayed a friend; they would stand severe punishment rather than give away a white friend who favored freedom for all.

There was a white man, Dan Kellogg by name, in Brunswick, who was a peculiar fellow and one I could never understand, and who I think was a northerner. For two or three years before the war he was known as a friend of freedom, among the slaves at least. He had told some of them so, and my impression is that as early as 1856, he told me that he was opposed to the institution of slavery, but of course this was *sub rosa;* but when the war broke out he had changed his mind and was classed with bushwhackers in that county, too much of a coward to join the Confederate Army and stand up in the open field to shoot and be shot at; but he hid in dense forests and shot at Union citizens and soldiers as they passed. I have been told that he was captured by one Captain Truman, commanding a squad of the Fourth Missouri Volunteer Infantry, and ordered to be hanged by the neck until dead, but was begged off by friends. I have not heard from Mr. Kellogg for many years and do not know whether he is dead or alive, but if he is alive and should read this statement he will, I think admit its truthfulness, May 20, 1893.

Since the above was written I have been reliably informed that Mr. Kellogg's death occurred about two years ago, and that he removed to Keytesville, the county seat of Chariton County, Mo., where he lived since the war, and had accumulated quite a little fortune and was up to the date of his death a staunch friend to the colored people, who greatly lamented his taking off.

He held the position of county treasurer for one or more terms, and regardless of politics, received almost the unanimous colored vote, he being a democrat.

CHAPTER IX.

The national election of 1860, created more excitement probably than any that had preceded it, not excepting the " Hard Cider Campaign " of 1840, because greater questions and issues had to be met and settled. The North was opposed to the extension, of slavery, in fact there was a strong sentiment against its existence, while the South wanted more territory for its extension; then there was a spirit of disunion existing North and South. The abolitionists of the North had declared the National Constitution to be a league with hell, while the extreme southern men such as Bob Toombs of Georgia, wanted to extend slavery to every State in the Union, and he declared in a speech delivered early in 1861, that he wanted to call the roll of his slaves on Bunker Hill, and would do so if the South was successful.

The campaign opened early in July that year, and kept red hot until the ballots were in the box. There was speaking once or twice a week at Brunswick, and several barbacues in different parts of the county. I remember attending one held five miles north of town, which appeared to be a joint affair, because there were speeches made in the interest of all the tickets except the Republican. My young master made his maiden effort for Bell and Everett, as I now remember.

The political excitement began in Missouri, especially in Chariton County, when the National Democratic Convention met at Charleston, S. C., April 23, 1860, and after spending ten days wrangling over the adoption of the platform, adjourned to meet at Baltimore, Md., June 18, 1860, without making a nomination for President. I might state that the main fight was upon the second section of the majority report of the Committee on Resolutions. The report reads as follows: Second, " Resolved, That it is the Duty of the Federal Government, in all its departments, to protect when necessary the rights of persons and property in the territories, and wherever else its constitutional authority extends." The minority report which was substituted for the majority by a vote of 165 to 138, reads as follows: " Inasmuch as difference of opinion exists in the Democratic party, as to the nature and extent of the powers of a territorial legislature, and as to the powers and duties of Congress, under the Constitution of the United States, over the institution of slavery within the Territories," Second, " Resolved, that the Democratic party will abide by the questions of constitutional law." After that vote many of the southern delegates withdrew from the Convention. Missouri stood solid in the Douglas column, refusing to secede with the other southern States, and cast her vote the following November for him for President and Johnson for Vice President.

If we stop to consider a moment, the fact that the Democratic party had the Supreme Court by a large majority at that time, we must arrive at the conclusion, that there existed no valid cause for the split in its national convention, thus dividing its strength and making it possible for the Republicans to elect their candidate; for it is generally believed that if there had been no split, Stephen A Douglas would have been elected

President and served his party as a good Democrat, for he owned a large plantation in the South, and the interest of the South would have been his as well. But it has always seemed to me that there was a higher power shaping matters and things at that time, which was irresistible. Hatred existed among Democrats North and South to such an extent, that southern Democrats denounced their northern brothers as " doughfaces " and cowards, which had the effect of driving many of them to vote the Republican ticket at the ensuing presidental election.

The extreme southern delegates who seceded from the National Convention, met and nominated John C. Breckinridge of Kentucky, for President, and Joseph Lane of Oregon, for Vice-President. From the day the campaign opened in the State of Missouri, especially in Chariton County, the two factions of the Democratic party were very bitter towards each other, and this condition of things existed up to and including the day of election, but when it was known later on that Lincoln was elected, all differences were healed and the factions came together, declaring for secession. They were joined by a large portion of the old line Whigs, who had voted for Bell and Everett at the last election; but there were a few who remained loyal to the Union. It is a wonder to me, even now, that they did so, when I recall the bulldozing, the taunts, jeers and epithets hurled against them. They were intensely hated and abused, more than the loyal Germans and northern men who had settled in that county, but they stood it out through trials and tribulations, remaining loyal to the close of the war.

There was another class of men who suffered

severely during the war, known as " Neutrals," assist-
ing neither side, but who were accused of aiding both
and therefore hated by both.

During the years of 1860 and 1861, the slaves had
to keep very mum and always on their masters' land,
because patrols were put out in every township with
authority to punish slaves with the lash, if found off
their masters' premises after dark without a written
pass from them. Patrol duty was always performed by
the poor whites, who took great pride in the whipping
of a slave, just as they do now in lynching a Negro.
They whipped some slaves so unmercifully that their
masters' attention was called to it, so that they met and
issued an order to patrols, that in punishing a slave
captured no skin should be broken nor blood brought
out by the lash. There being no positive law of patrol-
ling, it having existed as a custom to please a few mean
slave holders, many men whose names I can give,
would not submit to it, and threatened to punish any
man or set of men interfering in any way with their
slaves, although found off their lands. Of course the
patrols carefully avoided such men's slaves wherever
seen.

I have heard of many jokes played on these
patrols by slaves, tending to show how easy it was to
fool them, because they were as a rule illiterate, and
of course could not read writing. The slaves knowing this would take a portion of a letter picked up and
palm it off on them as a pass when arrested. The
captain would take it, look it over wisely, then hand it
telling the slave to go. Others would secure a pass
from their master, get some one who could read writing to erase the day and month, then use it indefinitely,

while others would get their young master or mistress to write them a pass whenever they wanted to go out, signing their father's name.

In order that the reader may clearly understand why slaves had to resort to so many tricks to get a pass, I will state that masters objected to giving passes often, upon the ground that they wanted the slave to stay at home and take his rest which he could not get if out often after dark.

In the fall of 1859 there was a dance given at Col. Ewing's farm, to which several young men and girls were invited and attended; most of them had passes except four girls, who had failed to secure them. The patrols came about twelve o'clock that night and surrounded the house, allowing those having passes to go free, and were preparing to whip the four girls who had none, right there in the presence of their beaux, who were powerless to protect them, when a young fellow, whose name was Lindsay Watts, came up and said, "Lor, massas, it am a great pity to whip dese sweet angels, 'deed 'tis; if you will let dem go, I will take the whippin' for dem all." His proposition was accepted, and the girls turned loose made rapid steps to their homes. The patrols took Lindsay outside of the yard, and stripped him naked, preparatory to giving him four times nine and thirty lashes, but being naked and hard to hold or grab, he escaped and ran home to his master in that condition, followed closely by the patrols. But his master protected him. The girls who barely escaped a lashing reached home safely and thankfully.

I remember another ball given a Day's Mill, near Brunswick, early in 1861, which I attended, and left about eleven o'clock that night. Later, a man named

Price, without law or authority, as he lived in the city and was not an officer thereof, gathered a squad of roughs and went to the Mill and surrounded the ball-room. They ordered all who had passes to come forward, and they were allowed to go free. There were five men and one girl without a pass left in the room. The white men stood in the doorway, intending to whip each Negro and pass him out. They had given the order for each one to take off his shirt. There was a fellow whose name, for prudential reasons, I will call John Smith, who got a shovel and threw fire coals, one shovelful after another, at the patrols. The lights had been extinguished; some of them got burnt in the face and neck badly, while others got clothing burnt. This cleared the way, and the Negroes, even the woman, escaped. They never found the man who threw the fire. I remember that they offered a reward to other slaves to betray the one who threw it.

About the winter of 1858, the Colored people gave a dance, to which many of the young people were invited and attended, and were enjoying themselves to their hearts' content, when, about twelve o'clock, a squad of patrols appeared and surrounded the ball-room. Those having passes were not disturbed, but those without were arrested and taken out for punishment, which numbered five, and of these only two were whipped; the other three resisted, and in the scuffle got loose and ran.

There was at that time a poor white man at the head of the city patrols, named Brawner, whose jurisdiction covered the city limits only, and he had no legal rights as patrol outside of it. But the desire of this poor white man to whip a slave was so great, that he left his post of duty, gathered secretly a squad of men of his ilk, went two miles into the country, and that, too, without the knowledge or consent of the city officers, for they knew nothing of it until next day. Now comes the worst part of it; when they had finished their hellishness, they returned to the city to find it on fire in several places, and as a result, several frame buildings in different portions of the city were destroyed by fire. Many efforts were made to detect the incendiary, but in vain, and the blame for the fire fell upon the Chief of Patrolmen, Brawner, who was, I think, promptly dismissed. I write of this matter without the fear of contradiction, because I am sure that there are men now living, white and black, who will corroborate my statement.

Slaves were much truer to one another in those days than they have been since made free, and I am unable to assign any reason for it, yet it is a fact, nevertheless, and as further proof of it, I will state, that they would listen carefully to what they heard their owners say while talking to each other on political matters, or about the fault of another slave, and as soon as opportunity would admit, go to the quarters and warn the slave of his danger, and tell what they had heard the master say about the politics of the country.

The Colored people could meet and talk over what they had heard about the latest battle, and what Mr. Lincoln had said, and the chances of their freedom, for they understood the war to be for their freedom solely, and prayed earnestly and often for the success of the Union cause. When the news came that a battle was fought and won by Union troops, they rejoiced, and were correspondingly depressed when they saw their masters rejoicing, for they knew the cause thereof. As I have stated before, slaves who could read and could buy newspapers, thereby obtained the latest news and kept their friends posted, and from mouth to ear the news was carried from farm to farm, without the knowledge of masters. There were no Judases among them during those exciting times.

After the war had commenced, about the spring of 1862, and troops of both sides were often passing through that county, it was not safe for patrols to be out hunting Negroes, and the system came to an end, never to be revived. The regular confederate troops raised in that and adjoining counties went South as fast as recruited, so that only bushwhackers remained, and they were a source of annoyance to Union men and Union troops of that county up to the fall and winter of 1864, when they were effectually cleaned out. Many of these men claimed to be loyal, especially so in public and at their homes in the day time, in order to be protected, while at heart they were disloyal, aiding bushwhackers not only with ammunition, rations, and information as to when and where Union troops would pass, but with their presence at night on the roadside, shooting at Union citizens and soldiers while passing. They would select some safe spot where a returned fire would not reach them.

The spirit of secession was almost as strong in that county in 1861, as it was in South Carolina, and when Fort Sumter was fired upon, Col. Pugh Price, of Brunswick, hung out the confederate flag, and called for volunteers. There were two companies raised who went South, one of which was commanded by Capt. J. W. Price. That county furnished its full share to the confederate army, composed largely of the best blood, men who were willing to shoot and be shot at in the open field of battle.

There was a man named James Long, a plasterer by trade, who was a noisy fellow, and who cast the only vote Lincoln received in that county. When called upon to give his reasons for so doing, he stated that he did it for fun; he then and there cursed Lincoln in language quite strong, and said that he ought to be assassinated. A year later, a loyal man had to be appointed postmaster at Brunswick, and then this man Long came forward as the only original Lincoln man, stating that his vote represented his sentiments, and that his former denial was caused by intimidation. He got the appointment, and in a year or two was arrested, tried, convicted and sentenced to the penitentiary for misappropriation of government money. But the secessionists lost a friend in him, because it was believed by Union men that he was not of them, and it was charged that he aided the rebels in every way possible, even to rifling Union men's letters, and giving their contents to rebels.

But this man's downfall was a blessing to some extent, to the Colored people who received mail through that office, for he would not give them their mail, but held it and delivered it to their masters Our family had no trouble in this respect, for our master would bring our letters unopened and deliver them without question. I remember getting one from my brother, B. K. Bruce, who was in Lawrence, Kan., at the time of the Quantrell raid, in 1863, which he brought from town, and waited to hear how B. K. Bruce escaped being killed in the Lawrence massacre.

From 1862 to the close of the war, slave property in the state of Missouri was almost a dead weight to the owner; he could not sell because there were no buyers. The business of the Negro trader was at an end, due to the want of a market. He could not get through the Union lines South with his property, that being his market. There was a man named White, usually called " Negro-trader White," who travelled over the state, buying Negroes like mules for the southern market, and when he had secured a hundred or more, he would take them, handcuffed together, to the South. He or his agents attended all sales where Negroes were to be sold without conditions. The sentiment against selling Negroes to traders was quite strong, and there were many who would not sell at all, unless forced by circumstances over which they had no control, and would cry with the Negroes at parting. A Negro sold to a trader would bring from one to three hundred dollars more money.

I recall a case where a master was on a note as surety, and had the same, which was a large sum, to pay at maturity, and to do so he was forced to sell a young girl to raise the cash. He sent for Negro-trader White, and the sale was made in the city without his wife's knowledge, but when he attempted to deliver her, his wife and children clung to the girl and would not let her go. When White saw he could not get his Negro, he demanded a return of his money, which the seller had applied on the note and could not get back. The matter was finally settled in some way; at any rate the girl was not sold, and was in that county until 1864.

The Negro trader usually bought all Negroes who

had committed murder or other crimes, for which public whipping was not considered sufficient punishment.
Slaves usually got scared when it became known that
Negro-trader White was in the community. The
owners used White's name as a threat to scare the
Negroes when they had violated some rule. "I'll sell
you to the Negro trader, if you don't do better" was
often as good or better punishment than the lash, for
the slave dreaded being sold South, worse than the Rus-
sians do banishment to Siberia.

Excitement, such as I had never seen, existed not
alone with the white people, but with the slaves as
well. Work, such as had usually been performed,
almost ceased; slaves worked as they pleased, and
their masters were powerless to force them, due largely
to the fact that the white people were divided in sentiment. Those who remained loyal advised the slaves
who belonged to those called disloyal, not to work for
men who had gone or sent their sons South, to fight
against the government. Slaves believed, deep down
in their souls, that the government was fighting for
their freedom, and it was useless for masters to tell
them differently. They would leave home in search of
work, and usually found it, with small pay, with some
Union man, and often without pay for weeks at a time,
but his master had to clothe him as he had always done,
and in some cases pay his own slave for his work.

Near the close of 1863, the Union men were on
top, and the disloyal or southern sympathizer had to
submit to everything. The lower class of so-called
Union men almost openly robbed rebel sympathizers
by going to their farms, dressed and armed as soldiers,
taking such stock as they wanted, which the owner was

powerless to prevent; in fact he would have been killed had he attempted it. The period had been reached when the master found his slave to be his best and truest friend, because it often happened that he was forced for self-protection to hide his valuables from these prowlers, and knowing that their quarters would not be invaded, he placed his precious property in their hands for safe keeping.

I remained on our farm, managing it as I had done in past years, but I saw that the time had about come when I could do so no longer. I saw men, whose names I could state, take from our farm hogs, cattle, and horses without permission and without paying for them, under the pretence that it was a military necessity. Of course no such necessity·existed, and the government received no benefit therefrom.

I remember that W. B. Bruce owned a fine lot of horses and cattle in 1862, but by March, 1864, they had all or nearly all been taken, without his consent, and often without his knowledge. I speak of only two cases of this kind, because I have personal knowledge of them. After the war, many of these men who had lost their property, other than slaves, presented claims against the government for property supposed to have been confiscated or appropriated to the use of Uncle Sam, and these claiments were honest in their belief that their property was so taken, when, as a matter of fact, it was taken by thieves, dressed in uniform for the purpose of deception, men who were not in the Union army, and the stolen property was used for their own personal benefit. W. B. Bruce is now living and can, if he will, testify to the truthfulness of what I state here.

The Germans were all Union men, and on that account had suffered severely at the hands of the bush-whackers from the beginning of the war to January, 1864, after which time they were as secure as any other class, and finally became the leaders on the Union side. W. B. Bruce and my owner joined their fortunes with the men of the South, and lost all they had contributed. Agents stole through the lines from the South, authorized to recruit men and receive money donations. They told wonderful stories about the confederacy, its success, what it would do, etc ; that they needed money and men, and in a very short time the war would be over, and the South would be on top.

I remember a young man named Kennedy, raised in Brunswick, and enlisted as a private in 1861, who went South in a Missouri rebel regiment. He came back in the fall of 1863 with the rank of Colonel, authorized to raise men and money for the southern confederacy. He was hiding around Brunswick and vicinity for a long time, and left without the Unionists knowing he had been there. Many southern sympathizers contributed money to the cause, which they have had dire need for since, and I believe my master and W. B. Bruce were among the victims.

I had several talks with my young master, W. E. Perkinson, in 1862, on the subject of loyalty. He wanted to join Col. Moberly's company of State militia, and if left to his choice, would have done so, but he was so bitterly opposed by his father and uncle, that he finally went South and served to the day of surrender, came home penniless, and with health gone. I am satisfied that he has sincerely regretted his action ever since, because he found young men, who were not his equals in ability and standing, but who had taken the

Union side, occupying important positions in the city, county and state, while he was disfranchised and did not get his disabilities removed for many years. He had been reared in the lap of luxury, graduated from college, then had studied law, and never earned a dollar to defray expenses; and he returned to find his father dead, his Negroes freed, and stock stolen, but the land was there, and that alone constituted his earthly possession. I was his playmate and nurse in childhood, though but a few years older, and always liked him; we never had any harsh words at any time, even after he had become a man. I have been informed that he has succeeded as a lawyer and judge on the bench.

There were a few poor whites who failed to identify themselves with either side, and of course did not enlist in either army; .they were anything to suit present company. Near the close of the winter of 1863–4 the Union side seemed to be getting on top, had a company of soldiers stationed at Brunswick, had rid the county of bushwhackers and rebel soldiers, and these fellows who had been on the fence for two years now openly declared for the Union.

CHAPTER X.

The enlistment of Colored men for the army commenced in Chariton County, Missouri, early in December, 1863, and any slave man who desired to be a soldier and fight for freedom, had an opportunity to do so. Certain men said to be recruiting officers from Iowa, came to Brunswick, to enlist Colored men for the United States Army, who were to be accredited not to Missouri, but to certain townships in Iowa, in order to avoid a draft there. I am unable to state the number of Colored men who enlisted in that county during the period from December, 1863, until the close of enlistments in the spring of 1865, but I am sure it was large. I had some trouble with these enlisted men, which was as follows: Being in the United States service themselves, they thought it no more than right to press in every young man they could find. Being secretly aided by these white officers, who, I learned afterwards, received a certain sum of money for each recruit raised and accredited as above described. These Colored men scoured the county in search of young men for soldiers, causing me to sleep out of nights and hide from them in the daytime. I was afraid to go to town while they were there, and greatly relieved when a company was filled out and left for some point in Iowa.

Our owner did not want us to leave him and used every persuasive means possible to prevent it. He gave every grown person a free pass, and agreed to give me fifteen dollars per month, with board and clothing, if I would remain with him on the farm, an offer which I had accepted to take effect January 1, 1864. But by March of that year, I saw that it could not be carried out, and concluded to go to Kansas. I might have remained and induced others to do so and made the crop, which would have been of little benefit to him, as it would have been spirited away. I made the agreement in good faith, but when I saw that it could not be fulfilled I had not the courage to tell him that I was going to leave him.

I was engaged to marry a girl belonging to a man named Allen Farmer, who was opposed to it on the ground, as I was afterwards informed, that he did not want a Negro to visit his farm who could read, because he would spoil his slaves. After it was known that I was courting the girl, he would not allow me to visit his farm nor any of his slaves to visit ours, but they did visit notwithstanding this order, nearly every Sunday. The girl's aunt was our mutual friend and made all arrangements for our meetings. At one of our secret meetings we decided to elope and fixed March 30, 1864, at nine o'clock, P. M., sharp, as the date for starting.

She met me at the appointed time and place with her entire worldly effects tied up in a handkerchief, and I took her up on the horse behind me. Then in great haste we started for Laclede, about thirty miles north of Brunswick, and the nearest point reached by the Hannibal and St. Joe Railroad. This town was occupied by a squad of Union Troops. Having traveled over that country so often, I had acquired an almost perfect knowledge of it, even of the by-paths. We avoided the main road, and made the entire trip without touching the traveled road at any point and without meeting any one and reached Laclede in safety, where we took the train for St. Joe, thence to Weston, where we crossed the Missouri River on a ferry boat to Fort Leavenworth, Kansas. I then felt myself a free man.

I learned soon afterwards that Jesse Boram, Allen Farmer and as many other men as could be hastily gotten together started in pursuit of us, following every road we were supposed to take, and went within six miles of Laclede, hoping to overtake us. Of course they would have ended my earthly career then and there, could they have found me that night. But I had carefully weighed the cost before starting, had nerved myself for action and would have sold my life very dearly had they overtaken us in our flight. How could I have done otherwise in the presence of the girl I loved, one who had forsaken mother, sister and brothers, and had placed herself entirely under my care and protection.

I am satisfied, even now, that I was braver that night than I have ever been since. I was a good shot and knew it, and intended to commence shooting as soon as my pursuers showed up; but it was a Godsend to all concerned, and especially to myself and bride, soon to be, that we were not overtaken; for I was determined to fight it out on that line, as surrender meant death to me. I had buckled around my waist a pair of Colt's revolvers and plenty of ammunition, but I feel now that I could not have held out long before a crowd of such men, and while I might have hit one or two of them, they would in the end have killed me.

My bravery, if that was what affected me, was not of the kind that will not shun danger, for I resorted to

every scheme possible to avoid it. We had the start
of our pursuers about an hour, or in other words the
girl was missed from her room in that time; then it
took probably another hour to get the men together.
But they stood a very poor show to capture us on the
main road, for we left it after the first half mile and
took to the brush and by-paths. They expected to
overtake us on the main road, where they would have
killed me, taken the girl back and given her a severe
flogging, but they were badly fooled, for we traveled
east, nearly on a straight line for six miles, then turned
north, the correct course of our destination.

I had heard it whispered among his Colored people, that Mr. Farmer's house was a kind of
rendezvous for the bushwhachers in that part of the
country, a place to meet to secure rations, amunition
and information, and that, occasionally, he went out
with them at night. If it be true that he acted with
brushwhackers, then I assert that he went out with
them just once too often, for he was killed as such, during the Summer of 1864, while on the run after being
halted.

As already stated in a preceding chapter, I had
learned to read, but could not write. Prior to leaving
home I printed with pen and ink a note, which was
pinned to the bridle, telling a friend of my master, who
lived within four miles of Laclede, and in whose front
yard I tied the horse about daybreak, to whom it
belonged, and requesting him to send it home or notify
its owner to come for it. I learned afterwards that the
horse, " Old Fiddler," was sent home the next day. I
did not want to be called a horse thief, and ever afterwards be afraid to visit my old home, friends and
relatives.

In January, 1865, I visited my old master and found him greatly disheartened and hard pressed. He told me that he wished I had kept the horse for he would have been better satisfied, as it had been taken from him by the thieves, dressed for self-protection in the uniform of Uncle Sam. He had but one horse on the farm at the time of my visit, and offerred that to me as a gift, knowing that it was only a matter of time, when it, too, would be stolen. I did not accept the gift and was sorry that I did not, for I was informed by letter that three armed men appeared a few days afterward and took, not only the horse, but a wagon load of corn to feed it.

CHAPTER XI.

On March 31, 1864, I landed at Leavenworth, Kansas, with my intended wife, without a change of clothing and with only five dollars in cash, two of which I gave Rev. John Turner, Pastor of the A. M. E. Church, who united us in marriage in his parlor that day. I knew a friend in that city, who came from Brunswick, Paul Jones, and upon inquiry soon found and secured room and board with him. The next day I was out hunting for work, which I obtained with a brick contractor, at two dollars and seventy-five cents per day, to carry a mud-hod, which I had done before; so that the work was not entirely new, nor the contractor a stranger to me. His name was Amos Fenn; he had worked for a contractor named Hawkins, who built a row of brick buildings at Brunswick, Mo., in the Fall of 1854, where I worked a few weeks, and when we met I remembered him and he gave me a job.

For the first few weeks I was well pleased with the pay I received, and thought I would soon have plenty of money, but now I had a new problem to solve, which was to support and clothe myself and a wife and pay doctors' bills, which was something new to me. I had never been trained in the school of economy, where I could learn the art of self-support, as my master had always attended to that little matter from my earliest recollections. Now I had expenses to meet of every kind The necessaries of life were all very high, including house rent, and by the time I paid up my bills on Saturday night, I found my week's earnings well nigh gone; this was the case right along. I also found that I had to make my own bargains for whatever necessaries we needed, and to provide for a rainy day, all of which experiences were new to me, yes, very new, and were a source of annoyance for a long time, because it taxed my mind each day to provide the necessaries for the next week and from week to week. I had lived to be twenty-eight years old, and had never been placed in a position where I had occasion to give this matter a single thought, for the reason that my master had it to attend to, as before stated.

I found myself almost as helpless as a child, so far as managing and providing for personal welfare and the future was concerned, and although I had been trained to work from a child and had acquired almost a perfect knowledge of it, together with a will and ability to perform hard manual labor, yet I had not learned the art of spending my earnings to the best advantage. I had a very limited knowledge of the value of any article, and often paid the price demanded without question, and ofttimes bought articles which were useless to me. My wife and I had good health and worked steadily every day, and by so doing managed to save up money enough in a short time to rent and fit up a small two-room house.

Continuing to enjoy good health and obtaining steady work, we had saved enough money within two years to buy the house and lot, paying nearly two-thirds cash therefor. I felt proud, being then for the first time in my life a land-owner, but it was of short duration. I had relied upon the word of a white man, and had paid him the amount agreed upon, and had received what I had supposed to be a clear title to the land, but it turned out soon afterwards, that the man owned only the house, and the land upon which it stood was the property of another, who notified me to pay rent for the land or move my house away

I found the white men of Kansas quite different from those of Missouri, in their dealings with Colored people or ex-slaves. They would talk and act nicely and politely, and in such a way as to win my confidence; always referring to my former condition and abusing pro-slavery men, pretending great friendship for me, and by so doing they ingratiated themselves into my confidence to such an extent, that I would follow their advice in the purchase of what they had to sell. Of course I believed what they told me and was often cheated out of my hard earnings

I had been reared where it was a crime for me to dispute a white man's word, and that idea was so well and thoroughly grounded in me that it took time and great effort to eradicate it. It took me a long time to learn that a white man would lie as quickly as a black one, and there are thousands of illiterate ex-slaves now living who have not entirely dismissed that idea, that a white man can not lie, drilled into them from early childhood, for I have found this true in dealing with them.

Let any ex-slave, uneducated, wanting information come to an educated colored man for it, and obtain it, he will not be really satisfied until he lays the matter before some white man, and if approved, then it is allright, but if condemned then the white man's opinion is accepted and the other rejected; this holds good to-day, and in my opinion is one of the results of slavery, which I can only explain by stating that slave-holders considered it very low to lie to a slave, and would not do it under any circumstances, and had great contempt for another one who would purposely do so. I have known them to refuse to answer questions rather than tell a lie, when they could not afford to tell the truth. Many times the slave has wished that his master would lie, when he has told him that at a certain hour or upon a certain day he would punish him; for he knew he would get the promised flogging almost as surely as the day came. Sometimes he would be told, " I am doing this only to keep my word." My own personal experience is, that in dealing with slaves the master was perfectly honorable and truthful, and would not cheat or practice deception in any way with them, and the slave knew that the master would not lie and therefore believed what he said.

I found by sad experience that the white men in a free state, especially in business transactions, were not as truthful as the slave-holders of Missouri, in dealing with colored people, a fact to which many colored men in Leavenworth and Atchison, Kansas, can testify, men like myself who have been deceived into buying a lot, and who, in installments had paid the entire price agreed upon. After having built a house thereon, in a few years they found that the land was owned by some one else.

I could give the names of several colored men in the cities named above, who lost their property in that way, and who were forced to vacate or pay a higher price for the land than at first. Men from the South tell me that that class of white men in that section, who were almost the soul of honor, in dealing with the colored people, is fast dying out, and the young men taking their places will lie to and cheat the ex-slave of his earnings right along, and do not display the honor of their fathers in such dealings.

I am unable to vouch for the truthfulness of this statement, not having lived in the South and therefore having no personal knowledge on that point. If it be true that the young men of the South, who have taken their fathers' places, are less honorable, less reliable in dealings with their fathers' ex-slaves, cheating and by deception, defrauding them of their earnings, then I assert that it is a sad reflection upon the once boasted chivalry and honor of the southern gentlemen, the men of the old school. But I am of the opinion that the class of men in the South, who are cheating and lying to colored people, are the newcomers and oldtime slave drivers or their offspring, who were always the enemies of the slave, and to day are jealous of him as a free man, and will take the lead in any matter that will militate against the colored man.

In thus describing my own experience upon being emancipated from slavery, I only show that of over four million others. History does not record where four millions of people had been held in slavery so long, that they had lost all knowledge of the way to provide for their own support, to expend their earnings to advantage, to use economy in purchasing necessaries of life and to lay up for another day.

This was the condition of the Colored people at the close of the war. They were set free without a dollar, without a foot of land, and without the wherewithal to get the next meal even, and this too by a great Christian Nation, whose domain is dotted over with religious institutions and whose missionaries in heathen lands, are seeking to convert the heathen to belief in their Christian religion and their Christian morality.

These slaves had been trained to do hard manual labor from the time that they were large enough to perform it, to the end of their lives, right along, and received no education or instruction in the way of economy. They had no care as to the way they were to get the next meal, the next pair of shoes or suit of clothes. This being the duty of the master, they looked to him for these necessaries, just as a child looks to its mother or the horse to its master for its daily sustenance.

The history of this country, especially that portion of it south of Mason and Dixon's line, shows that the labor of these people had for two hundred years made the country tenable for the white man, had cleared away the dense forests and produced crops that brought millions of money annually to that section, which not only benefitted the South, but the North as well. It does seem to me, that a Christian Nation, which had received such wealth from the labor of a subjugated people, upon setting them free would, at least, have given them a square meal. Justice seems to demand one year's support, forty acres of land and a mule each.

Did they get that or any portion of it? Not a cent. Four million people turned loose without a dollar and told to " Root hog or die! " Now, whose duty was it to feed them? Was it the former masters' or that of the general government, which had conquered the masters, and in order to make that victory complete freed their slaves? My opinion is that the government should have done it.

The master had been conquered, after fou years' hard fighting, and largely by the aid of the two hundred thousand Colored volunteers, mustered in the United States Army, and told to fight for the freedom of their race. The history of that conflict says they did it loyally and bravely.

General Lee had surrendered. The South had staked its all upon that contest and had been conquered and laid waste, as it were; its business gone, its crops confiscated by both armies, and its slaves set free, but it had to feed these homeless and penniless people or see them starve. No one will say the masters did not feed the freedmen until a crop was made, and, too, at a time when they had no money in cash and no credit at the North.

When we take into consideration the penniless condition of these four million people at the close of the war, and the fact that they were destitute of education and turned loose in the midst of a people educated in science, art, literature and economy, a people owning the land and chattels of every kind, with money to do the business of the country and with the experience and training of a thousand years, the fact that the freedmen did succeed under these adverse conditions in obtaining a living, and in many cases in getting little homes for themselves and families, instead of becoming a public charge, is greatly to their credit.

Many white people who were friendly to them had great mis-givings and doubts as to whether these freedmen could succeed in making themselves self-supporting in the race of life, with so many obstacles to meet and overcome. They were illiterate, without money and confronted with a prejudice due in part to their former condition and in part to the fact of their being candidates for the labor work, which, up to that period, had been performed by the poor whites, especially foreigners, in the North, East and West.

The freeing of the American slaves and their partial migration to these states, seeking employment, excited the enmity of the white laborers, particularly the Irish, because at that time they constituted fully seventy-five per cent of the laboring class, and who imagined that the influx of Negro laborers from the South, would divide the labor monopoly which they held, and of course they became opposed to the Colored people and so much so, that they would have done almost anything calculated to extirpate them. They were always ready to incite a riot and take the lead in it, and had not the business men, capitalists and ministers frowned upon their course, would have succeeded in doing serious harm.

I remember the bitter feeling existing between the Irish and the Colored laborers in Leavenworth, Kansas, which had its beginning about the close of the war. They had several little conflicts, and on one occasion the civil authorities interfered to prevent bloodshed.

I recall an instance when the Colored people had been informed that the Irish were intent on surrounding the Baptist Church, corner Third and Kiowa streets, to " clane the nagurs out," on Sunday night. The Colored people prepared to meet them, by selecting Fenton Burrell as captain, and secreting nearly fifty armed men in a vacant lot in the rear of the church, to await the appearance of the Irish. Soon a squad of them came up Third street to within a hundred yards of the church, but after halting a few minutes marched back and dispersed. I learned afterwards that Col. D. R. Anthony, a recognized friend of both races, went in person to the leaders and informed them of the reception they would receive if they proceeded further, and advised them to disperse and go home, which they did.

The Negro has committed no offense against the Irish; the two races had never lived together at any time to engender hatred, and as I understand it, there is no valid reason why the Irish should have been so bitter against the Negro, except the fact that they were both seekers after the unskilled labor of this country. I have stated that it was the labor question that excited the enmity of the Irish against the Colored people, and the reason why I say this is, that the past history of the two races since the conquest of Ireland, by England is much alike; both had been in bondage a long time. While the Irish had not been in slavery, pure and simple, they had been held in a state of subjugation and servitude, nearly approaching to it, and enjoyed but few more liberties than the American slave. They had a country only in name and no voice in the government thereof or ownership in the land on which they lived, any more than the slaves in the United States They were not free men until they reached the United States. With such a similarity in past history and present condition, it would seem that these two races should have been friends instead of foes, and in my opinion they would have been, had they not been seekers for the same kind of employment, and thus becoming competitors. So that the scramble for that employment has caused the Irish to resort to means, which have aided largely in kindling the feeling of prejudice against the Colored people. They were aided in thus accomplishing this object by the native poor white, and the further fact that they were white men, because whenever that question or issue is raised, it will catch the illiterate whites en masse, and in many cases the thoughtless aristocratic class, who will join a mob to lynch a Colored man without giving the matter a second thought, as to whether he is guilty or not. In many cases the charge is cooked up for a sinister purpose, to get rid of him, or in order to obtain a lucrative position held by him.

I have stated before that it is the labor question, more than any other, which causes the Colored people to suffer greater indignities than any other class of Americans in this country, and I believe it is not on account of their color, so much as it is the desire of white laborers to do the work and to receive pay which might go to him It is an admitted fact that these same laborers or mechanics in search of a job, will go South, where the Colored men have charge of such work, or nearly so, and will not only work with them, but hire to them and be bossed by them. Foreigners, seeking employment, have gone to the South in large numbers during the last five years, and finding there the typical poor whites, who are the ancient enemies of the Colored people and ever ready to do them harm, have united with them on the color line and raised that old familiar cry that "this is a white man's country, that white men must and shall rule it; no Negro domination over white men." When that feeling has grown sufficiently strong to cover the real designs of the vicious elements, and to deceive the better class, then it is that the charges against some harmless, helpless Colored man are trumped up, and they lynch him. So rapid is the mob in forming and blood-thirsty in its murderous howls, that the better class is powerless to assist the helpless victim while alive, and when dead the charges which were preferred by a poor white man or a foreigner, for a mere trifle or sinister purpose, are magnified until it would appear that the victim was a savage brute and deserved the punishment inflicted. So brutal are these charges made to appear after the death of the victim, that the better class of southern white people, allow these lynchers to escape punishment, upon the ground, I suppose, that they had rid the community of a bad character.

The lynching of the Colored people is always the work of the poor white laboring class, and as a striking incident tending to show the facts, I call attention to the list of the killed and wounded at Roanoke, Va., in September, 1893, when the State militia, in upholding the dignity of the law of the State, fired into a mob, killing and wounding thirty men, twenty-four of whom were laborers, track-walkers, section hands, and employes in the machine shops of that city. I take these figures from the published report made at the time of the occurrence; and to my mind one thing is made plain by this incident, which is this, that it was not the aristocracy that was doing the lynching at the South, or any other part of the country, though they are held morally responsible in the eyes of the nation.

But the aristocracy of the South is getting its eyes open to this growing evil, and I am of the opinion, that its eyes will not have been opened any too soon, for this is only another form of anarchy, which is feeding itself upon the Colored people, and will ere long turn upon the aristocrat and the capitalist, and serve them even worse than the Colored people have been.

The better class at the South will soon see the error of their past conduct, if they have not already done so, in taking the poor whites into their confidence and social circle,' which, I suppose, was for political purposes, for they now feel themselves the equals of their former lords, and will not down at their bidding. They drove out the Republican government at the South by brutal force, and they had the acquiescence of their former lords, who enjoyed a benefit for a time, but this element of roughs, augmented by the influx of foreigners, is beginning to show its disloyalty to the old aristocratic element by leaving them at home, and when possible, sending one of its ilk as a representative to the legislative halls, State and National.

But as to lynching, I think I see among the better class evidence of a change of public sentiment taking place at the South, a return to law and order, as indicated by a few extracts from leading newspapers in that section. The first is from the *Indianapolis World* (Colored), issue of September 19, 1893, as follows: " It looks as if light were breaking into the hitherto darkened condition of the South. The carnival of crime in which the depraved and merciless element of that section has reveled unchecked for many months, is at last arousing the dormant spirit of justice and fair play, inherent in the American bosom, and the fabric upon which our Constitution rests. Just as the insolent and exorbitant ambition of the slave power laid the train, which resulted in the downfall of the unfavorite institution, the repeated cruelties, tortures, and human outrages of southern brutes has awakened the conscience of the better classes, whose love for the fair name of their country outweighs all fear of Negro

domination. The 'vaulting ambition' of the stake-
burners and lynchers has overstept itself, and we verily
believe the reign of misrule is reaching the beginning
of the end."

A few months ago, scarcely a southern newspaper
dared to lift up a voice against the inhuman practices
of the mobs. They either gave open encouragement
to their so-called " best citizens," or silently acquiesced.
To-day, however, the leading journals of Virginia,
South Carolina, Georgia, Tennessee and Louisiana,
perceiving the change of the tide, and that the southern
craft is dashing dangerously near the breakers of
anarchy, are pleading for a cessation of horrors, and
the re-establishment of law and order. The *Memphis
Commercial* has been at all times one of the most arro-
gant and ungenerous enemies of the Negro throughout
the South, but it is a revelation of a highly creditable
character to hear it give birth to such sentiments as
these: " Even when outraged virtue and all the ties of
nature and humanity call for the death of criminals, the
demoralization of violence and the contagion of cruelty
accompany these things. There is no passion which
so thrives from gratification as the lust of cruelty. The
English Parliament declared that public executions
were debauching the whole British people. Mercy
was drowned in blood during the reign of terror, and
the whole future of French civilization is stained and
poisoned by the memory of the guillotine. So it is with
lynching in the South. The horror has spread, and a
people, originally the gentlest, bravest, noblest in the
world, are actually threatened with a generation of
cruel and violent men. Every boy, who witnesses a
lynching, loses something of his humanity. Every

groan of the dying wretch kills part of his native tenderness, and every drop of blood congeals the mercy and gentleness of his heart. It were better that a young man should cut off his right hand than to see the torture of one man. It is better that he should be struck with deafness than to hear the death shriek of one dying ravisher.

"Such scenes have made the Murats and Robespierres of history. Such things done in America will curse the future of civilization and darken the glory of coming years. Hence, we deem that swift and summary justice should be meted by law to all who practice these horrors, unless the flagrancy of the offence justify lawlessness by the higher law of necessary punishment. In Louisiana, a few day ago, a mob of brutal whites most cruelly lynched three innocent Negroes, and have sent word to the agents of the State's laws that they intend to burn another one in broad daylight. This constitutes treason, and we hold that the Governor of Louisiana should stamp it out at once, if it must be done with the bayonet of armed authority. It is the glory of the South, up to this time, in spite of all that may be said to the contrary, that she has been considerate, generous and kind in the face of the most difficult class of conditions that ever confronted a people. Let us not lose so fair a fame by any delays of laws or fears of prejudice."

These sentiments are their own comment, and indicate that if the appeals of the Negro for justice for justice's sake are ignored, the southern leaders are learning that they cannot escape the consequences of natural laws and are moved to action through the law of self-protection. The strong stand taken against mob violence by Governor Brown of Maryland, Governor McKinney of Virginia, and the ringing words of brave Mayor Trout of Roanoke, are all encouraging cases in point, which evidence the change of front by the intelligent, thrifty and liberty-loving people below the Mason and Dixon line.

We must not lose our head, or fly into an impotent rage when contemplating our wrongs. Let us recognize fully the seriousness of our condition, study the temper of the southern mind, analyze the cause of every action against us, and set about applying a sensible remedy, based upon the state of the case as shown by the symptoms. A condition which is the natural outgrowth of slavery will improve as the evils of that period diminish. Therefore let us grow in education, in wealth, in respectability, in morals, and in political generosity, and we will rise to our rightful place in the esteem and confidence of the nation. This will take time, and time is an essential element in the solution of all chronic complaints and in all great problems.

Before closing this chapter, I feel that an explanation should be made as to what I really mean in using the term " poor white " people, for I do not want to be understood as meaning that all poor white people are alike, and therefore are opposed to the Colored people's enjoying the rights and immunities conferred upon others by the law of the country, for such is far from my intention or desire. There are thousands of aristocratic white people who are poor, financially speaking, due to accident or misfortune, but they still retain in their veins the blood of aristocracy, that will not and cannot be concealed by the change of position. This class, as a result of the war, is more largely found in the South, but wherever found, as a rule, they always are the friends of the oppressed, and the Colored people regard them as their friends.

Blood and education will tell; even the children of that class of men are infinitely superior to those of the typical poor whites, whose offspring seldom rise above the positions held by their fathers' in life, and when we find one who has, we regard him as the exception, and not the rule. He may acquire wealth, and, on account of it, command respect, but will have all the failings and prejudices of his kind or line of consanguinity.

Now as to the Irish, I do not want it understood from what I have said concerning the position they have occupied toward the Colored people, that they are all enemies to the ex-slave, for such is not the case, because there are thousands of them in this country as friendly to the Colored people as any other class of American citizens, and just as ready to give them a fair show as any other.

But I will state, that my experience has been that this class of Irish Americans are the refined, educated class always, and not the common laborer, or the illiterate class. But I think I see a great change for the better taking place.

The Irish who have been in this country long enough, and are educated, and have accumulated money, are giving up the labor work, and engaging in the various kinds of business, leaving the labor work to be performed by others, and in such cases they cease to be prejudiced. The Germans have never sought the labor work of the country, and therefore have always been friendly with the Colored people, and retain their friendship and confidence in return.

CHAPTER XII.

I have stated in a former chapter that the Colored people, notwithstanding the many adverse circumstances surrounding them, did succeed in obtaining a living and avoided becoming a great public charge, which fact, I think, will be universally admitted But we can go further and show that they not only accomplished this, but other things, equally as great during the period from 1865 to the present. Many white people believed, when these people were freed that they were incapable of taking education, and therefore could not safely attain to citizenship, all of which has long since been shown to be erroneous, and at this present time the men holding such views cannot be found.

The Colored people have fully demonstrated their ability to take education, not only in the common, but in the higher branches as well, and as rapidly and as thoroughly as the white student. They have also shown their ability to master any of the learned professions, so that the men who have heretofore prated so loudly about the incapacity of the colored man, have been driven successfully from each stand they have taken, until the last ditch is reached; they now admit the Colored man's ability to cope with them in the professions, but say he is unreliable. But he will soon drive them from that position also.

We are now classed as a " Negro " race. Webster says the word " Negro " applies to black men of southern Africa, or their descendents.   While there are a few pure black men among the Colored people of the United States, at the most, not over one-fifth, the other four-fifths are mixed, in a lesser or greater degree, with the white race, and this process of mixing has been going on for over two hundred years. Children take their nationality from their mothers and not their fathers; so that every child whose mother is a white or a Colored American, is an American to all intents and purposes, and cannot be otherwise. These mixed bloods married, and begat children, who were Americans. Though they were deprived of their liberty by American law, they could not be called Africans any more than the white Americans could be called Europeans, and this forces me to state that there is no such a thing as a Negro race in this country. We are Colored Americans and this, I think is the proper name for us.

One thing is pretty clearly seen, and that is, we are not a race with sufficient race pride and affinity, which are the special prerequisites of all races of men in the great struggle for race supremacy. We have not and cannot have race pride, because we know nothing of a mother country; nothing of a united people; nothing of the different nations in Africa, from which some of our ancestors were purchased or stolen. We are here by the will of God, and He will in His own time and in His own way shape our destiny. For the present, in my opinion, we are here to show the sin and wickedness of the American people, and we are herr to stay. This is our country; our coming here being co-existent with that of our white brother, we know no other; we have contributed our full share to make it what it is; we have defended it in all its wars, before and since the

Declaration of Independence, and we will defend it against all nations. We are Americans as truly as any others in this land; this is our home, and its flag is our flag.

I have been unable to find a case in history, ancient or modern, where a people had been held in subjugation and ignorance so long, and reduced to such a state of immorality, that they had not the slightest conception of, or respect for the marital relations, and especially the moral law. This was the condition of the Colored people at the close of the war. It is unnecessary for me to ask, who was responsible for this crying shame, or whether it was the fault of the Colored people. In my opinion it was and is the sin of the American people, who had gone to Africa and stolen little children from their virtuous homes and parents, brought them here, reared them as they reared their cattle, and regardless of the rights of humanity, the laws of morality and Christianity itself, reduced them to slavery, and robbed them of all conceptions of chasity and virtue. I have said this crime was committed by the American people, and I say this, because nearly every one of the original thirteen States, which formed the United States, July 4, 1776, held slaves or recognized property in them. But the most absurd of all absurdities, is to hear white people prating about the immoral conduct of Colored people when, as a matter of fact, they are responsible for whatever they see in us to condemn, for we are what they made us. I say Colored people, because we would have been pure black, were it not that immoral white men have, by force, injected their blood into our veins, to such an extent, that we now represent all colors, from pure black to pure white, and almost entirely as the result of the licentiousness of white men, and not of marriage or by the cohabitation of Colored men with white women.

The fact is this, that we had to take ourselves as we found ourselves, regardless of the many different shades of colors among us, and start then, for the first time in our history, to build our own characters and homes, with a very limited knowledge as to the way to proceed. Upon being emancipated we commenced the practice of morality and virtue by going to the church and the courts, and being legally married, and by raising our children up in the care of the church and the Sabbath schools. So that in a very short time after our freedom, nearly all those who had been living as man and wife, by order or consent of their masters, had been lawfully married. Then and not till then, did we commence to build our own homes and to perpetuate a name. Of course the name could be only that of our masters, as we had none and were compelled to adopt that of our last master or some other, as the names that were borne in Africa, by our stolen ancestors, were entirely lost, after nearly two centuries in slavery.

It should not be expected that a people with so many disadvantages and drawbacks could attain to the degree of morality and virtue of a people, who had the benefit and experience of a thousand years' training, but I think we compare very favorably with that class of whites, who can command no more capital than we. Our people have not added to the increasing number of tramps, infesting nearly every State in the Union, committing crime wherever they go, and causing the women to be in mortal fear in the absence of their male protectors. The Colored people are, as a rule, content and faithful workers wherever employed, a fact which contractors who have given them work will confirm. They have never been known to organize a strike, or to be in any way connected with one, unless it be to accept work where white strikers had refused, and that at the solicitation of owners or contractors. So that it may be stated without the fear of successful contradiction, that the Colored laborers are the most reliable class of workers the country possesses to-day, less riotous, less turbulent and more tractable than any other class, and can and do perform as full a day's service.

The Colored American is most loyal to his government as a citizen and as a soldier, a fact which will be generally admitted by even his worst enemies. He is not to be classed among the anarchists, or any other class of men who plot against the laws of the land. His loyalty and bravery as a soldier have been shown, not only in the late war, but since as an enlisted man in the regular army, a fact which the Seventh United States Cavalry will admit willingly, because it was the Colored troops that came in the nick of time to their aid at the Wounded Knee fight, and turned defeat into victory. And speaking of their loyalty, I feel safe in making the assertion, that they would be among the first to enlist to defend the old flag, in case of an invasion by a foreign enemy, even though he landed his forces in the extreme South.

Having no mother country with which to divide his sympathies, the old flag would receive the Colored soldier's loyal support. Can this be truthfully said of any other distinct class of adopted citizens ? I think not. Suppose this country was forced to declare war against Germany or Italy, could we expect the undi-

vided support of the German Americans or the natural-
ized Italians ? ,Not at all. We would be at the mercy
of either of these great powers, because they could
have their spies and emissaries in our rear at every
movement. This would not be the case with the Colored Americans, who know only America, and whose
allegiance need not be questioned. The Colored
American will be found fighting in the ranks of the loy-
alists to sustain our present system of government in-
tact when the great conflict shall come, which now
seems threatening, and which came near being inau-
gurated at Chicago in the spring of 1894, between those
who are loyal to our present economic system of government, and the extreme socialists, who are mostly of
foreign birth, and therefore less in sympathy with our
institutions and established mode of government.

The Colored American will always be found voting and fighting on the side of the white American aristocratic classes, the classes that have made our common country what it is to-day—the best government on
the face of the globe, and who are striving to keep it
in the lead of all other civilized governments.

There are several questions of great magnitude
agitating the minds of the American people to-day,
questions which have been before them for the last few
years; and which will have to be met and settled, in
my opinion, at no very distant day, and in that final settlement, whether in a war of ballots or bullets, the Colored Americans will wield an important power, and
will have an opportunity to make themselves masters
of the situation.

When the social question, or the struggle between
labor and capital, between law and order, between

American and encroaching foreign ideas, shall present themselves for settlement, the Colored Americans, being most loyal to everything that is American, and especially to those things which conduce to law and order and good government, can and will always be found battling against the anarchist and the revolutionist of any character. On account of their unwavering loyalty to America and its established institutions, the Colored Americans will in such struggles, in all probability, hold the key to the situation, or the casting influence, and if rightly and wisely used, they will hold the balance of power in this country.

I have tried to show that the typical poor whites and their allies, the foreigners, seeking to control the labor work of the country, are no friends of the Colored people, and have never been, and that the Colored people cannot support any measure they may advocate. So then it will be seen that it is the duty of the Colored people to support the principles of the better classes of white people, North and South, for the aristocratic classes are our real friends, and are also the friends of good government for Americans.

I cannot see how a Christian nation can so far forget its duties as to allow a loyal, industrious class of its citizens to suffer injustice and wrongs at its hands, a class of people who only ask a fair chance in common with its other citizens. One great injustice the Colored people are forced to suffer, without the means of redress, is at the hands of the press, especially the periodicals, which allow any writer who may wish to attack the Colored people, space to vent his spleen, and when he has given his story about them, whether true or false, the publishers will not allow the Colored writer space to reply. Strange as it may seem, these publishers will promptly refuse to publish articles reflecting upon the moral habits and character of any other distinct class of people in this country. Then why treat the Colored people differently? Fair play and a fair show are all they ask, and this they will ever ask, and as Americans this they have a right to ask.

Great injustice has been inflicted upon the Colored people of this country by men engaged in business enterprises, such as manufacturers, mill and mine owners, in their refusal to give them employment. These great captains of industry have persistently discriminated against the sober, industrious, faithful Colored American citizen, and given preference to foreigners, who, neither understanding nor feeling the slightest interest in our institutions, have, at times, by strikes and boycots, caused great loss to the employer and the employed, and unnecessary inconvenience to the general public

I make no complaint against that class of men, who, leaving the old world and coming to the new, and assuming the responsibilities of American citizenship in good faith, adopt the broad American doctrine of equal rights to all. I refer to that irresponsible class, who, leaving their country for their country's good, have contributed little or nothing to the peace, order and prosperity of the United States; they are the inciters of strikes, riots and general disorder in nearly all of our great centres of population.

The situation in this respect is becoming more and more a matter of anxiety and alarm on the part of patriotic Americans, and the question now confronting us is, "What shall we do about it?" Many things can be done, some of which must be done speedily. Restrict imigration to the industrious, sober, law-abiding classes, enforce the law rigorously against rioters, anarchists, and the like, make education compulsory, and teach English in all the public schools, and admit to the factories, the mills, the mines, and other works, the worthy American worker, both white and Colored, upon terms of perfect equality.

It is a burning shame, a disgrace to the country, that our own citizens should be denied the opportunity of earning a livelihood at the suggestion of a herd of ignorant and lawless foreigners.

CHAPTER XIII.

The white people charge us with being imitators, incapable of originating anything in the domain of science, art or invention, and to a certain extent I am free to admit that the charge is true, and the reasons are easily explained Being a new people, as it were, we had not attained to the point of originality, and situated in the midst of white people who had education, refinement of manners, money and the advantage it gives, we are compelled to imitate them. Besides, it was their advice to us to do so if we wished to succeed, and we have, therefore, been imitating them for nearly thirty years, adopting their habits and customs, the good, and, I am sorry to say, the bad as well. Having followed the advice of those white people, who we knew meant well, and whom we knew to be our real friends, as anxious for our success as we were, and who will have our sincere thanks always, for the noble and generous deeds they have done for us; yet we have made mistakes. Whenever we could, we gave our children the same course of study that white children received, often graduating them from the same platform, and then, when able, sent our boys to college to take a professional course, either in law, medicine or the ministry, this being the usual course followed by white parents, and being imitators, could we be expected to adopt any other with our limited means or foresight ? I answer, no.

Being a peculiar, or I might say a proscribed people, the same course of study, after leaving the common branches, which was deemed best for the white children, experience has shown us, was not the best suited for the Colored children. Being almost entirely a laboring class of people, we should have used every means in our power to educate our children's hands as well as their heads by giving them a trade of some kind, by establishing industrial schools as a part of the course of study, so that our boys would have a trade when they reached the age of twenty-one years, and our girls at the same age coming out of the schools, would be trained nurses, cooks or seamstresses, prepared to make an honest living.

I do not want it to be understood that I am opposed to the higher studies or professsions ; far be it from me. On the contrary, I am proud of every young Colored man who has attained to these honors, and would be glad to see as many more turned out full-fledged every year. In order that they may take our places in the labor world, when we, who have been taught trades by our owners, shall have passed from life to death, we should strive to give our children trades of some kind, and we should commence now Have we to-day as many shoemakers, carpenters, bricklayers, blacksmiths, stone masons and wagon makers among us as when emancipated ? I think not. This presents a very unfortunate condition, if true, and I believe it is But I am glad to see our people awakening to this neglected duty, and I think no man deserves more credit for this than Booker T. Washington, President of the Tuskegee Normal and Industrial Institute.

On the fourth of July, 1881, this school began, in an old church building, with one teacher and thirty pupils. Since then its growth has been most remarkable. To-day it owns over 1500 acres of land, nineteen buildings, has more than six hundred students, forty-one teachers, and gives instruction in eighteen industries. Its lands and buildings are worth $185,000. Its industries include farming, brickmaking, sawmill work, planing, carpentry, painting, brickmasonry, plastering, blacksmithing, wheelwrighting, chairmaking, mattress-making, printing, bee-culture; and for girls, laundering, general housekeeping, sewing, including cutting and making garments, and cooking lessons for seniors. Eight of the largest buildings have been built wholly or in part by student labor. It has been the aim of the school from the first to combine thorough mental training with industrial work.

No one can visit the school to-day and see what it is doing in the class-room, in the farm, in the carpenter-shop, in the blacksmith-shop, in the sawmill, in the brickyard, in the printing office, in the laundry, in the sewing room, in the literary societies, and in the various religious exercises,—for the development of the head, hand and heart of the young men and women gathered there, without feeling profoundly thankful to God.

There are a few things about this school that are especially worthy of note: 1st. It is a live school. It believes in progress. It has never stood still a day since its organization. Every year it presents new evidences of growth and development. 2nd. It does what it aims to do thoroughly. It employs only well-qualified officers and teachers, and subjects all its pupils to the most rigid examination before sending them forth. 3rd. It is no sham affair, existing on paper

only.   It is all it represents itself to be, and more; and
it does all it professes to do.   4th. Its funds are wisely
and economically administered; there is no waste anywhere, everything is utilized, and utilized for the general good.   The immediate work to which the school
is committed, in its greatness and importance, seems to
weigh upon every mind; and how to get the most out
of what they have is the one thought.   Hence the sal-
aries are small and the working force is cut down to
the smallest possible number, thereby increasing the
burdens of the officers and teachers, but by them willingly, cheerfully endured, as it helps to keep down expenses; hence, also the buildings, as well as their fur-
nishings, the food, etc., are all of the plainest character.
An example of the rigid economy which characterizes
everything there, may be found in the fact, that eight
dollars will keep a young man there for a month, including everything, board, lodging, washing, mending,
fuel and light.   5th.   Every officer and teacher in it,
from the beginning to the present, has been Colored.
Whatever ability has been displayed therefore in the
management of its affairs, and in working it up to its
present high standard, we may justly claim as our own.
In this particular it stands alone among the Colored institutions in our land.   Not that there are no other
schools that have proved a success under exclusively
Colored management and direction, but none of such
magnitude, whose success is so unquestioned, and
where such large sums of money are expended annually.

The feeling of the whites in the neighborhood is
now most friendly to the school, and they frequently

employ the students in their different departments of
labor. As an illustration of this friendly feeling, a
southern lady living near the school has recently given
to it an estate valued at $15,000.

At the head of this school, and its animating,
controlling spirit, from the very beginning, is Prof.
Booker T. Washington, a graduate of Hampton,
a quiet, unassuming man, with a wise head and a big
heart, and the weight of this race problem resting upon
him as upon scarcely any other that I have met. You
do not hear very much about him through the columns
of the newspapers, or of his addressing great meetings
in the various parts of the country; but judged by his
work, he is a most remarkable man—a man to be
proud of, and to be honored, a modest man, caring
nothing about notoriety, content to be unknown, so long
as the work goes on, and his people go up ; a born
leader, with all the elements of leadership, especially for
the work in which he is engaged, with a keen intellect,
a strong will, courage, perseverance and enthusiasm.

When this great race problem shall be solved ;
when slavery and all its dreadful consequences shall be
a thing of the past, and when we shall stand on the
same plane with others in point of wealth, intelligence
and culture, which I firmly believe we will, and even
the history of the influences by which it has been
brought about shall be written, I believe that no man
will be assigned a more honorable place than this man,
Booker T. Washington.

I have written quite fully of the institution over
which Professor Washington presides, to the exclusion
of others, not because there were no others worthy of

mention, but because I had fuller information of that institution than of any other. But I am reliably informed that there are several such schools established in the South, and that they are doing a good work, but being in their infancy, as it were, are not on a par with the Tuskegee Institute.

CHAPTER XIV.

In a former chapter I have attempted to show the manner in which we have suffered in the past from the effects of an unwarranted prejudice against us, due not so much to our color as to our condition, and from the mistakes we have made in mapping out the course best suited for us to follow. We are a peculiar people, hitherto unknown to the laws of the United States. We have been made citizens by these laws, but are still regarded as a distinct people. In this chapter I shall try to give my views as to the best course for us, as a class, to pursue in order to succeed in the race of life as newly made citizens, and this advice is intended wholly for the Colored people.

Above every other consideration we must get money, and to do that, we must engage in business of some kind, however small, and then support it with our undivided patronage. By so doing we shall not only build up business houses, but create places for our boys and girls when they leave the schools, fitted for higher callings than the mudhod or the washtub. We can do this without any sacrifice, as we are compelled to spend a large portion of our earnings for the necessaries of life any way, and when it comes to the question as to whether we shall spend it with a white or a Colored tradesman, other things being equal, the question itself ought to suggest the answer.

We would do well, in my opinion, to take a few lessons from the Hebrews in this country, as to the way in which to accumulate money, for they have been sorely pressed by all Christian nations for centuries, and notwithstanding have steadily, and in the face of great prejudice, accumulated vast wealth. By turning their attention entirely to trade, they have been enabled to command respect by reason of their money solely, so that to-day, especially in this country, they have a very high standing in the commercial business of the country, and are gradually increasing it each year, so that it is only a matter of time, when they will be able to control such business. They give their children a common school course, then a business course, and then put them to work as salesmen, rarely ever sending them to college.

We are the real producers of the wealth of the country, especially of the southern portion, and have that advantage over the Hebrews, who never produce anything at any time, and yet they strive to control the business of the entire country. As an evidence of the fact that we are the real producers, note the large number of mercantile failures when there is a shortage in the crop. Now then, since we are the producers of the wealth, why not spend it in a way to benefit ourselves? So long as the merchant can get our trade without recognition, he will not give employment to our young men and women, in consideration of that class of trade, and is sometimes bold enough to say so.

As a case in point, I will state this: A few years ago, a certain merchant on Pennsylvania Avenue, Washington, D. C., who had and still has a large trade with the Colored people, especially the better class, including the families of clerks in the several departments and school teachers, there being over three hundred of them, was applied to by a delegation of Colored citizens for a position for a respectable and well-educated girl, wanting employment. They called his attention to the fact that he had a very large Colored patronage and that he had employees representing nearly every other class of people, and that it would be nothing more than fair to give employment to one Colored saleswoman. He refused. They gave him to understand that an effort would be made to withdraw the Colored trade from him, since he would not recognize it in a substantial way. His reply was: " Gentlemen, you may make all the efforts you please, but you cannot do it; good day "

Are we prepared to say that this merchant did not state the fact? I think not, because he knew our disorganized condition, our inability to concentrate our strength in a way to make it effective, and therefore felt free to tell the delegation to their faces, " You cannot do it." He spoke the truth, the whole truth, and nothing but the truth, because they could not do it then, and cannot do it now, and never will until the Colored people are educated to it by force of self-defence.

As parents we are partly responsible for the idleness and unemployed condition of our young men and women, after they have reached maturity and left the schools, by neglecting to utilize the means in our hands for the benefit of our children. After having given them an education which fits them for higher callings than mere ordinary laborers, we fail to create these higher places for them, and the children, as a matter of fact, have been injured rather than benefited by our misdirected kindness and parental love. To a very large extent this accounts for the great number of young men and women marching the streets in idleness, for which we are directly and morally responsible. We have no just cause for censuring the white people for their conduct toward us in refusing us recognition. They have done no wrong; they have only taken advantage of the opportunities we have given them and nothing more. They know that we are a disorganized people, and while in that condition are certainly not in a position to strike back when pressed, and therefore they press us with impunity.

It is not enough to say that the prejudice against us is due to color; while in part that might be true, there is another and a greater cause, which in my opinion, fans and keeps alive that hydra-headed monster, and that is our penniless condition. We are a class of people who represent, comparatively speaking, nothing, and in the business world absolutely nothing, although we are the producers of the wealth in several States, as has already been stated, we have no voice in the barter and sale of it.

The laws are made by and for the business men of all countries and not in the interest of the laboring classes. The business men are the law-makers in this country and of course shape the laws to suit their own interests. My candid belief is, that more respect will be shown us, when we are represented in the business world, and I think we should make an effort to be represented in the various lines of business as other Americans. We have tried various plans, looking to success, and have not attained it to a very satisfactory degree, and I think the time has come for us to try something new. If we were a distinct race, as some

writers who have not given the subject much thought
assert, the advice to make an effort would be super-
fluous, because being a race we would necessarily be a
united people, aiding one another in efforts to rise.
Circumstances compel us to be a distinct class of
Americans, without regard to shades of color; because
we have many among us who are as white as any Cau-
casian, but when the fact is known that they have in
their veins the slight admixture of African blood,
whether they are of light or dark hue, they are all
classed as Colored people, treated as such, and might
as well mingle as such, allowing character only to be
the dividing line. The fact is this, we are all Colored
people and must hold together as such, if we expect to
succeed, remembering that in union there is strength,
and the old adage which is a good one, that it is better
to be a king among dogs than a dog among kings.

I have thus far tried to show some of the causes
operating against our progress and the part we have
acted or taken against our own best interests, in our
blind efforts to succeed. And now as to the remedy.

Our ministers see the necessity of our being more
closely united in a business way. They picture the
good results that will follow such action, and like Rev.
Dr. Seaton, of Georgetown, D. C, heartily approve
such a course, and at the same time lay the blame for
non-action at the doors of our political leaders, by saying that they should have been advising, urging and
educating our people, up to this essential necessity long
ago. Our political leaders also see the necessity of
such action on our part, and have advised us, whenever
they had a chance to be heard, to be more closely
united, but they insist that little good can be accom-

plished until our ministers become interested in the
matter.   Here it is seen that both classes of leaders see
the need of and admit the necessity for such action, and
yet both remain comparatively inactive.   Not being a
minister or a political leader, I feel myself competent
to decide this question without prejudice and therefore
state that, in my opinion, it is the failure of our spiritual
advisers to discharge their whole duty towards their
congregations, and I will mention some of my reasons
for making this assertion.   In the first place our ministers wield a greater influence over the people than any
other class of men, and can if they choose, lead them
into almost any measure they may wish them to adopt.
They have led them to contribute of their meagre earnings, the large sums of money invested in church property, located in every State.   It was raised by the
untiring efforts of our spiritual advisers, a little at a
time; so that it is claimed that the Colored people of
the United States, own over two hundred million dollars worth in church property, and support fifteen
thousand ministers, at an annual cost of seven and a
half million dollars a year.*

By the payment of such a large sum annually,
without a murmur on our part, it would seem quite
reasonable that we are entitled to and should have not
only the spiritual, but the temporal advice as well, for
we need it badly   Again, our ministers are always in
touch with their congregations and see their needs,
have their undivided attention whenever desired, talk to

---

* The above figures are furnished by Rev. F. J. Grimke,
of the Fifteenth Street Presbyterian Church, Washington, D. C., from
which I make the estimate of five hundred dollars as the average cost of
each minister, which I think very reasonable.

them, selecting their own subjects every week, about saving souls, and the course they should pursue to accomplish that desirable result. All this is very good, and they love their pastors for showing them the way to eternal life, but it seems to me that while the ministers have their ears, confidence and continued attention, and knowing their divided and thereby weakened condition, should, if they have any genuine pride in them, take advantage of their position and give them some instruction as to the caring for the body, as well as the soul. If they will do this, as though it were really a religious duty, advising them mutually to aid one another with their patronage, they will have rendered their people a lasting service.

There is hardly a doubt, that our ministers have an advantage over our political leaders in this; they have the people before them every week, and therefore have a better opportunity to advise and urge them towards united action, than the political leader, who may not have a chance to address his people more than once or twice in a year, and that at some celebration. I am decidedly of the opinion that the various religious bodies in this country, supported by us, should instruct their ministers and see that they carry it out, to devote more time to the temporal care of their congregations, by teaching and urging upon them the necessity of being more closely united as a people; that in union there is strength; that a house divided against itself cannot stand. Our ministers can unite us, and they alone can. Will they make the effort?

Those among us who have accumulated wealth have done so single-handed and alone, and against great odds, and in nearly every case by dealing with

white men, rarely with a majority of Colored custom-
ers. I cannot recall a single instance where a Colored
merchant, relying solely upon the patronage of his own
people, has succeeded. That old idea drilled into them
during slavery, that white people are better than Colored people, is still in them, notwithstanding their
denial of the fact, for it is shown in their actions, in the
purchase of what they need and in the employment of
skilled workmen. If the job is a small one, amounting
to a few dollars, we may give it to a colored workman,
but if it is a large one, we give it to a white man, who
will then send, probably, the Colored bidder to do the
work, and we are satisfied. And as to our purchases,
we act as though the white man's goods were better than
those of the Colored man. In this respect the upper
as well as the lower classes of Colored people need
training badly, a fact which many of us, who are now
or have been in business will confirm.

When we are ripe for it, there will appear Colored
men with means ready to enter nearly every line of
business, who are now afraid to do so, because of the
fact that they cannot rely upon their own people for
support.

We recognize three distinct grades among us;
namely, the wealthy or those who have acquired money,
supporting their families in the style that aristocratic
Americans do; the working class including those
engaged in business, professors, tradesmen, and the
daily laborers; the third and last class includes the
shiftless, worthless, and thoroughly degraded. Many
prejudiced white people affect to know but one grade,
and that the lowest always, and promptly charge all
crimes committed by that class to the Colored people

generally, taking that class as a criterion by which to judge the entire people, placing men like Frederick Douglass on a par with this degraded class, in speaking to him about them as "your people." They know as well as they know anything, that Mr. Douglass has no more dealings or association with that class of Colored people, than Chauncey M. Depew has with the roughs and thugs of New York. It really makes me feel hurt to hear white men who, I believe, know better than to talk that way, men who will never reach Mr. Douglass's standing, if they live to be old as Methuselah.

It would be well for us to remember, that we cannot always be considered as little helpless babes, and therefore objects of charity by the white philanthropists of this country. They have been very liberal towards us in their donations to establish institutions of learning, not only in the common branches, but the higher as well, so that we have a large number of colleges and universities sustained by donations from the white people, regardless of politics. We own many million dollars worth of school property, located in the South, which came to us by donation, besides a large amount invested in church property, much of which came in the same way. The charitably-disposed white people of this country have been very good to us, but we are now nearly thirty-year old children, and these philanthropists will find that out some day and cease their liberality upon the ground, that we are old enough to take care of ourselves. Can we dispute this fact? I think not. We will have to meet the obstacles I have referred to at no distant day, and should be paving the way to that end, so as to be prepared for them when the time comes. If there is a better plan than the one I have suggested, one more practical, let it not be only stated, but adopted and put into active operation, for we cannot expect to succeed with so many difficulties, as we are now forced to encounter, unless we unite ourselves more closely.

In addition to present obligations as members of our several religious creeds, we should have one obligation, pledging our support and patronage to each other in preference to any other class. As already stated, we are morally and religiously responsible for the conduct and character assumed by our children in after life. If as parents, we have discharged our whole duty towards them, and have complied with divine instruction in accordance with Proverbs xxii. 6: "Train up a child in the way he should go, and when he is old he will not depart from it," we need have no fear as to our childrens' success in after life.

One almost neglected field of labor in which our ministers should spend more time and attention in their efforts for reform, and one which is in the line of their special calling, is this: A very large number of supposed Christian people, members of churches, in most cases in good standing, entertain and practice a false idea of the virtue of prayer, believing honestly that it is the panacea for every evil, and cure for ever wrong committed, even intentionally. They believe that any crime committed against the law of the land, or any violation of the laws of God, can be atoned for by prayer; or in other words, they believe that they can steal the goods and chattels of another, and without making restitution go to the Lord in prayer, and that he will forgive them and allow them to retain the stolen goods. Among the illiterate class of Colored people, this false idea or misconception of divine law is practiced entirely too much. Our ministers should turn their attention to the eradication of this evil practice or false conception of the word of God In a large degree, in my opinion, this accounts for the great number of church members, in good standing, before the police and other courts, charged with petty larceny.

There is another evil practice which is closely allied to the one above described, and needs the attention of our teachers and preachers badly. It is this, religion without morality. We have too many immoral religionists in our churches. There are members of our churches apparently filled with religion, as it were, and at the same time totally devoid of morality. I can conceive of a moral man without religion, but I cannot conceive of a religious man devoid of morality.

Among the illiterate and also the shiftless class of Colored people these seeming incongruities exist, and herein lies work for our educated ministers and our Christian teachers to show the right. We want pure men and women, honest, upright, reliable, and trustworthy in every station, and to obtain them we must raise up our children correctly, or in other words, we must raise them up to be truthful and relf-respecting. The young man or young woman possessing these qualities will succeed even in adversity, for these traits of character will be of incalculable benefit to them in obtaining and filling responsible positions.

With the aid of our ministers, the reforms I have mentioned can be obtained, and our ministers will have made themselves our leaders in fact, and we will have been placed under renewed obligation to them, and will also be placed in a better condition to respond to their support than we have been in the past. Will they undertake this great reform, and continue to persevere until their efforts shall be crowned with success ? I hope and pray they will.

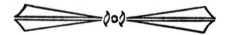

CHAPTER XV.

In this closing chapter I shall try to give more of my personal history than has been stated in the preceding ones; for in those I spoke only of matters and things as I saw them, and incidentally mentioned the wrongs we suffered, the causes leading up to them and the remedy. But in this chapter, as stated above, I shall confine myself more closely to my own personal history and experience.

By the winter of 1867–1868, I had, by hard work and strict economy, since the close of the war, saved up five hundred dollars, with which I bought out a small business fronting on the levee at Leavenworth, Kansas, and made money out of it from the day I took possession. I immediately had improvements made to the extent of two hundred dollars, and thought I had a bonanza. Being located in an old frame building, I could get but two hundred dollars insurance on my stock, and it was good that I got that much, for within sixty days from the time I bought the place it was destroyed by fire, with its contents. I had the two hundred dollars only. I then secured another location, and with the assistance of the firm of Haas & Co., merchants of that city, I was partly on my feet again, although in debt to them for my stock of merchandise. I succeeded in paying off my debts and getting a fair living out of the business, and continued it until the fall of 1870, when I transferred it to Atchison, Kansas, where I still continued in the same business until the fall of 1875, when it, too, was destroyed by fire, entailing a loss of six hundred dollars. I then rented the brick building on the corner of Fourth and Commercial streets, owned by Hon. C. C. Burnes, and opened again, and continued the business until the fall of 1878, when I was forced to close for want of cash. I had bills due me for groceries amounting to thirty-three hundred dollars, which I could not collect, due in part to two causes: a very severe winter, and the very dry summer which followed, in which the farmers' crops were entire failures. My liabilities were about one thousand dollars, which I could not meet, and was forced to the wall. I have never been able to collect over ten per cent. of those bills, which are now dead by limitation of statutes.

About this time I found myself without money, and had a wife and four children to support. A friend advanced me money enough to buy two express teams, one of which I drove, and the driver of the other was paid one half of the cash he collected. I made a fair living out of that business, repaid the borrowed money, and had some cash on hand, when I received the Republican nomination for the Legislature from the Fourth Legislative District of Kansas, in the fall of 1880. After a hard fought campaign I was defeated by Hon. George W. Glick, by twenty-five votes, out of a total of nine hundred and fifty. That defeat was a very severe blow to me, because I had spent, in what is called legitimate election expense, every dollar that I had saved up.

Soon after the day of election, business grew very dull, and winter set in early and was very severe, so that from November 6, 1880, to January 10, 1881, I experienced the hardest time I ever saw. I had a family to support and my mules to feed, as they did not earn money enough to buy their feed By the efforts of Senators L. M. Briggs, A. S. Everest, J. W. Rector, Ira Collins, Richard Blue, and others, I was elected Doorkeeper of the State Senate, January 10, 1881. That election was a Godsend to me at that time, for I was hard pressed for cash, so much so, that I did not have money necessary to pay my fare to Topeka, to be sworn in, and I borrowed ten dollars from Colonel John A. Martin.

The pay was twenty-one dollars per week, which amount carried me through the winter, and to the close of the session.

After the adjournment of the Legislature and my return home, General W. W. Guthrie secured for me the position of foreman of a gang of forty-two Colored men to work a construction train on the A. & N. Rail Road, between Atchison, Kansas, and Lincoln, Nebraska. The salary paid me was fifty dollars per month. I promptly accepted the position, and held it until August, 1881, when my brother, who was then Register of the United States Treasury, telegraphed that he could get me a position in the Post Office Department, at Washington, at a salary of seven hundred and twenty dollars per annum, with a chance of promotion. This I considered a permanent job, and one less dangerous, and I accepted it and came on to Washington.

After one year's service in the Money Order Division of that Department, and no promotion or prospect of one, my brother secured an appointment for me in the Pension Office, at the salary of one thousand dollars per annum, and I was sworn in, September 22,

1882, as an examiner, which position I have held ever
since. I was promoted to Class One in the fall of 1886,
and to Class Two in the summer of 1889. Of course,
I appreciated these honors, and felt proud of them,
probably more than some other men would have done.
And why should I not, when I recall that I was a slave
at the age of twenty-nine years, then freed without a
dollar, could not write my name at the close of the war,
but by close study since then, had reached these positions ?

Having served under every Commissioner who
has held the office of Commissioner of Pensions since
September, 1882, and having had a good opportunity
for observing the administration of the office by each,
candor compels me to state, that General John C.
Black filled that chair with more dignity, ability, and
impartiality, than any of those under whom I have
served. He held no "Star Chamber" investigations.
If one clerk preferred charges against another, he was
required to put them in writing, signing his name; then
the accused was furnished a copy of said charges, and
given a chance to be heard in his own defense before
action was taken. If unable to meet and refute said
charges, then, and not until then, was action taken.

General Black was Commissioner in fact, when he
occupied that position, and no underling was allowed
to dictate to him his duty. No clerk, high or low, republican or democrat, could leave his desk at will, and
go to have a chat with the Commissioner, without first
obtaining a written permit to do so. I am sorry that I
cannot say the same of others under whom I have
served.

General Black had no pets; every employe was

required to perform his duty without favor and irrespective of party or color. He broke up the rings which had existed in the office, whereby some got easy places, little work and big pay, came to the office when they pleased, and left it when they felt like it

Up to the beginning of General Black's term of office, examiners had been rated according to the number of pension claims submitted, either for admission, rejection or special investigation. Gun shot wound claims were always considered as easy cases, much more so, than injury or disease claims, and an examiner who was lucky enough to draw from the files a bundle of the former class of claims had an advantage over his fellow clerks, who drew the latter class, because these gunshot wound cases required very little work to complete them, while the other classes would require three or four times as much work, and often covering from one to seven years time in which to obtain the necessary evidence to establish the claim I recall an instance, when I saw a chief of divisons go to the files, select a bundle of gun-shot wound claims, bring them to a certain examiner's desk, lay them down, smile and walk away. Of course, that examiner gained an advantage over others by the action of his friend.

Soon after assuming charge of the office, General Black issued his famous order, number 110, whereby all employes were required to be at their desks at nine o'clock, A. M., and at one o'clock, P. M., thirty minutes being allowed for lunch, from twelve thirty P. M., and to remain at their desks, until four o'clock, P M., when the office closed. Chiefs of divisions were required to see that order strictly enforced, and to report all violators of it, to the Commissioner immediately, and he would require the violator to write him a letter, explaining the cause of tardiness. If the excuse given was satisfactory to the Commissioner that ended it, if not, the violator received a severe reprimand through letter, directly from the Commissioner. So that order number 110, cured tardiness effectually in the Pension Office, and that order remains in force to-day and notwithstanding the great number of orders now in force, every employe has perfect knowledge of old order, number 110.

Up to the spring of 1885, when said order was issued, many favored employes failed to appear at their place of duty on time. Some were thirty minutes, and some an hour late; some would leave the office one, and sometimes two hours before closing time, and this would occur quite often during the month. These same employes would apply for their thirty days annual leave and obtain it, just the same as those who had not been tardy.

Order, number 110, has been modified in form some what, but its essential parts are still in force and will remain.

Promotions under General Black's administration of the Pension Office, were based upon merit solely, and with respect to Colored men it was eminently so; for they were Republicans and had no special claims upon a Democratic administration, and yet I am informed that there were more Colored men promoted under that administration than under the one following it. Of course, with other Colored employes, I was quite scared, when the Democrats carried the country in 1884, thinking that we would all be discharged, and when we were not, we were very agreeably surprised.

Many white Republican leaders wished it, and some were bold enough to say that the Colored man would have to go. Among those who said it was Ex-Senator Ingalls, who stated to me, that he wished the Democrats would discharge all Republican office holders. I understood him clearly. He meant it as an aid to solidify the Republican party vote at the polls. By the failure to discharge the Colored employes, the thing the Republican leaders most desired, the Democrats made many friends for their party, and particularly President Cleveland.

Mr. Cleveland's election in 1884, and assumption of power in March, 1885, however much they regretted it, was a good thing for the Republican leaders, because they had on hand a lot of old barnacles to care for, as chiefs of divisions and the like, who, occupying those positions, were a dead weight to the party, and they had held them so long, that rings had been formed, whereby none but its members or their friends stood any chance of promotion, however worthy they might be. These rings were so well organized, that they could and did defeat the endorsements of Senators and Members of Congress. When the change came and these leeches had to step down and out, and new men appointed fresh from the people, of different views and politics, with no pets, no favorites and free from ring rule, and whose only duty or desire was to see the work over which they had charge faithfully performed, then it was that every employe was required to attend strictly to his duty, and every one was placed upon a common level.

Some of these deposed chiefs, on account of old age and as a matter of charity, in some cases, were reduced to clerkships and allowed to remain; but even then it was hard on them, to be forced to come down to do clerical work with men whom they had lorded it over, and in some cases treated unjustly while in power. But after all, the service was purified by the change, and when the Republicans came to power in March, 1889, they appointed in nearly every case new men from the States to these chiefships, who were free from rings and cliques, and they ignored the claims of the old ex-chiefs, who thought they had a monoply of these positions, and were bold enough to say so when speaking of them, as " my old place."

Of course, the Colored employes were benefited by any change, that put all on a common level where no favors were shown, and each one was credited with the amount of work done and nothing more. I have seen men who had been of the favored class before the change, working hard and close to retain their present pay in the higher grades to which they had been promoted over others more deserving. Some of this class of employes were reduced to a lower grade, and some by hard work and promptness to duty retained their pay in the higher grades

My reference to rings relates to the Pension Office exclusively, but I have been reliably informed that the system obtained also in other bureaus and depart ments, especially the Treasury.

Hon. James Tanner, who succeeded General Black, as Commissioner of Pensions, was an able man and also a good man, and one liked by employes regardless of politics; and I believe, would have suc- ceeded in the administration of the office of Commis- sioner of Pensions, with entire satisfaction to the

country, had he surrounded himself with strong men as
advisers.   But he failed to do so and failed as Commissioner, not because of his inability to discharge the
duties of the office, a fact which can be proven by his
previous official life and subsequent conduct, as an
attorney before the various departments of the Government, but solely because of falling into the hands of
weak advisers.

Mr. Tanner in turn, was succeeded by Hon. G. B.
Raum, a man of details and rules, who reminded me of
what an English correspondent of a London paper,
who was with our army during the late war, wrote of
General McClelland, to his home paper, after seeing
the General himself superintending the laying of a pon-
toon bridge across some river, an act which any ordinary army officer could have done with ease. The correspondent said that General McClelland was a man of
details, spending his time, which should have been
devoted to a higher calling, on matters of minor details,
which are the duties of subordinate officers, and therefore could never be a great general.

General Raum, would have been a *great* success
as general superintendent of the working force of the
office, seeing it done well and adopting rules best
suited for its accomplishment. He acted the part of
superintendent well.

There are chiefs and assistants in every division.
A chief clerk and assistant, a captain of the watch, and
a superintendent of the building. With this large list
of officers, one would suppose, that any order issued
could be carried out to the letter, without the personal
attention of the Commissioner, but such was not the
case. He could be seen almost any day giving his per-

sonal direction to the divisions, just as though he had
no officer in ' charge competent to carry out his orders.
He visited every part of the building, even to the wash
rooms; for I have seen him in those rooms abusing the
laborers about the spittoons, etc., not being clean, thus
ignoring his captain of the watch, whose special duty
it was to look after such work.

General Raum had no pets or favorites to award
easy places, and I think that he was a man who really
wanted to see every employe doing his duty. He
worked hard and wanted others to do the same.

With his record before us as General of Volunteers, Member of Congress, and later on as United
States Internal Revenue Commissioner,—all of which
positions he filled with eminent satisfaction to the
country,—can any one doubt for a moment General
Raum's honesty and ability? I think not.

His administration of the Pension Office, while it
was not up to the high standard attained by General
Black, was the equal of any other under which I have
served, and had he relied more upon his subordinates to
attend to the minor details of the office, and devoted
his entire time to higher questions of law governing
pensions, his administration of that office would have
been much more esteemed.

Commissioner Raum was succeeded by Judge
William Lochren, the present incumbent, who, like
General John C. Black, belongs to that class of men
who disdain to do small things and whose likes and dis-
likes of men are not based upon their color. Therefore,
he, like General Black, also fills the chair of Commissioner of Pensions with dignity and ability. Exhibiting
confidence in the ability of his subordinate officers, to

effectively carry out his instructions, the Commissioner relieves himself of the ,objectionable duty of going from room to room to watch the employes.

Judge Lochren is a disciplinarian and insists upon a strict compliance with the rules laid down for the government of the working force of the Pension Office, and allows no favoritism to be shown any employe regardless of politics, sex or color. All are required to perform their full duty.

A man whom I regard as thoroughly reliable, informed me that he was present and heard what was said at an interview between Commissioner Lochren and a certain chief of a division in the Pension Office, who had recommended a Colored man employed under him for dismissal, without any cause assigned or charges preferred against him. It appears that charges of dereliction of duty, inefficiency or insubordination had been filed against several employes and after an investigation, three or four of these employes were recommended for dismissal and the papers for the same were prepared and laid on the Commissioner's desk for his signature. By some means, not explained, the recommendation for dismissal of a Colored man whose name I shall designate as Mr. L., got with the other papers, which had been agreed upon for dismissal for *cause*, and Commissioner Lochren approved, and then sent them to the Secretary of the Interior, who also approved them, and those employes were dismissed in a few days thereafter, Mr. L., in the lot. Immediately upon receiving his notice of discharge, Mr. L., sought and obtained an interview with the Commissioner of Pensions. During this interview it became clear to Mr. L., that the Commissioner had no personal knowledge of his case. Mr. L., then presented his certificate of discharge and politely asked to know the cause for which he was dismissed. Being unable to state the cause, the Commissioner asked Mr. L., to leave with him his certificate of discharge and to call next day, which he did. Pending this conversation, the Commissioner sent for the division chief, who made the recommendation for Mr. L's. discharge, and demanded of him the grounds upon which he had recommended this man's dismissal. He could only state that he did it in order to get a place for a Democrat, and upon being further questioned, he admitted that there were no chargss against Mr. L., that he was a good man and had discharged his duty satisfactorily. After hearing his reply, the Commissioner turned to this chief, very abruptly, and said: " How dare you recommend a man for dismissal against whom no charges have been preferred? I want you to understand that this thing must not occur again, and that I will have Mr. L., reinstated immediately."

It is needless for me to state that Mr. L., was reinstated within five days from that date and is now on the pay rolls of the Pension Office, drawing his little stipend of nine hundred dollars per annum.

It sometimes happens that a *small man* gets the position of chief of a divison, and by reason of the fact that he has none of the aristocratic blue blood in his veins, but comes from the lower class of white people, and is therefore filled with the prejudice of his kind, he will try hard to get rid of Colored clerks under him, by means which are very questionable. Cases of this kind are rare, but they have occurred under Republican as well as Democratic administrations and I state this, because I have been hearing of such cases during the last fourteen years. Such white men are in all political parties and whenever elevated to power over Colored men, will deal them a blow in the back when they have the opportunity to do so under cover.

Now as to dismissals, reductions and promotions, they have occurred under every administration following a change of political control. They occurred during President Cleveland's first term and again under President Harrison's administration, and it is quite reasonable to expect them to occur under the present regime; *because the party in power, will always find some means by which they are enabled to place their political friends in good places.* It was the practice under Republican rule, and it is the practice under Democratic rule and, in my opinion, it will always be the custom, not only in the Pension Bureau, but in all the departments of the government, even at the expense of reducing their opponents to lower grade in pay.

Of the one hundred and twenty-five Colored employes, borne on the pay-rolls of the United States Pension Office, on November 7, 1892, there was only one man who claimed to be a Democrat, and he hails from the South and was then, and is now, a $1400 clerk There were four or five Colored employes, who opposed President Harrison's renomination, but when he received it they quieted down like good party men, but after Harrison's defeat, they commenced to trim sail, as it were, and by March 5, 1893, they had become fullfledged " After Election Democrats."

So as a matter of fact, we had no special hold upon a Democratic administration for favors in the shape of promotions. There were one hundred and twenty-five Colored men on the pay-rolls of the United States Pension Office, March 5, 1893, and there are now, March 30, 1895, borne on said rolls, the names of one hundred and twenty-three Colored employes, showing that we have lost only two men since the Democratic party regained control.

The records of this office show the following:

Number of Colored employes on the rolls March 5, 1893:

Clerks - - - - - -	92
Labor Roll - - - - -	33
Total - - - - -	125

Number of Colored employes appointed since March 5, 1893:

Clerks - - - - - -	1
Labor Roll - - - - -	18
Total - - - - -	19
Number of clerks discharged - - -	7
Number discharged from Labor Roll -	14
Total - - - - -	21
Number of clerks reduced - - -	20
Number of clerks promoted - - -	8
Number now on rolls - - -	123

Among the twenty clerks reduced, from a higher to lower grade of pay, my name occurs, but as it was a political matter purely, and did not reflect upon my efficiency as a clerk, and only reduced me from fourteen to twelve hundred dollars, I felt that there was no cause afforded me to grumble and did not do so. And although being one of the unlucky number, I am free to say, that Colored employes have been fairly treated thus far, under Judge Lochren's administration, and so far as my own personal treatment goes, I can say truthfully, that I never received more respect and kindness under any administration, than I have under the officers of this, from the Commissioner down to my section chief.

Like most people in the States, who have only a vague idea of a clerkship in the departments of the government at Washington, I thought a position in one of these departments was a bonanza, and that I could save at least one half of my salary every month, and that any clerk who did not do so was a spendthrift, and ought not to be retained. I soon learned that nearly everything one needed costs more here than the same article would cost in the States, besides, one is almost compelled to board and room at a first class place, and pay a higher rate for whatever article he needed, in order to be classed with respectable people. If one stopped at a cheap house with second-class people, that act alone settled his status in Washington society.

There are private and public boarding houses here, which furnish room and board at from twelve to forty dollars per month, so that one can take his choice as to place and price, but the usual price paid by Department clerks for room, board and washing, is about twenty-five dollars per month. A decent house here, with modern improvements, cannot be rented for less than twenty-five dollars per month, nor a front room for less than ten dollars for the same period. One will soon find that he must dress in the latest style, if he wishes to be on a par with his fellow clerks, and to do that he is required to go dressed up in his best clothes every day, thereby making his clothing bill twice or three times what it would be in the States. Of course, there is no regulation requiring clerks to appear at their desks dressed in their best clothes, but there is an implied understanding, that poorly dressed employes are to be classed with the lower grade of Washington society, a position not desired, because it is generally believed that a clerk who is too stingy to spend money so as to appear at his desk decently dressed, is not a fit subject for promotion. At any rate, in my opinion and experience, such persons seldom, if ever, are recommended for a higher grade, and what I state here applies to lady clerks and gentlemen alike.

So that a new clerk from the States, receiving an appointment here, thinks for the first few weeks that he is going to save money, and not only that, but he is going to set an example of ecomony to his fellow clerks. But he soon finds that he cannot do it, and if he would command respect and association, he must do as he sees others do, and like an adept, he falls in, convinced that his fellow clerks are not spendthrifts after all. There are several other lessons the new clerk learns, after he is sworn into the Departmental service, especially if he came in through examination under Civil Service Rules; that there are old clerks here, who are competent to teach him many things which he failed to learn at school, and that the ideas he had previously formed, touching the ability of government clerks, who were appointed prior to the passage of the Civil Service Act, were erroneous. To his surprise, he finds men and women in the Departments here,

highly cultivated and well posted in the very latest literature of the day, and competent to take a leading
part in almost any of the historical and scientific re-
searches of recent date. So that the newcomer,
although having successfully passed a civil service examination, and received an appointment based thereon,
must take his position at the foot of the class, as it
were, and go to work to even hold that position, for it
has often happened that such clerks have been dropped
after six months service—" cause, Inefficiency," while
older clerks, because of their efficiency, hold on.

One of the first lessons a new appointee should
learn, and I might say the most important one, is entire
and complete subordination, for without this he cannot
succeed. He must make up his mind to lay aside
what he calls his manly instincts and personal independence, and resolve to submissively obey all orders
of his superiors without a murmur, even though they
are not stated exactly in accordance with the rules of
syntax, laid down by Lindley Murray. He will also
find that he must so act as to win the respect and confidence of his superiors in office, and to so live as to
hold them, and to do this, he must be a gentleman
away from the office as well as in it, for if he keeps bad
company, the report of it will eventually reach his superiors, and thereby affect his standing materially. A
new clerk will not be here very long before he will find
that in addition to these other necessary requirements,
that " Influence " counts a good deal, and without it
one can make slow headway singlehanded and alone,
trusting to his own ability. To obtain social standing
and influence, one must associate with the better class
of people, and to do that he must be of clean character,

if he expects to obtain *entre* therein.   The various Departments of the government here are run by old and
experienced clerks, who have spent a large part of their
lives in this service, and cannot well be displaced by
the new ones, however intelligent they may be.   The
fitness of these old clerks is proved by long, efficient
and faithful service.   They also very clearly understand
the value of influence, and know just when, where and
how to bring it to bear.   They are regular diplomats.

But aside from other considerations; these men
have devoted their lives to the service, grown old in it,
and are content, and I might say, fitted to this kind of
work to the exclusion of all other work.   They cannot
go out into the world and make a decent living on their
own wits, and therefore should be let alone, because the
government has received the benefit of their best days
of service, and should not cast them out on account of
old age, at least, to " go over the hill to the poor
house."

THE END.

ENDORSEMENTS.

Probably the most unique work of its kind will be Mr. H. C. Bruce's book, "The New Man." It is ostensibly the author's autobiography, but he has made more of it than a simple narrative by interweaving with his own experience much of the history of the antebellum days and very many vivid descriptions of the habits and customs of the Old South

One of the most conspicuous features of this book is the entire absence of the passion usually displayed when former slaves refer to their past bondage. Yet without this very dispassionateness no history can be authentic. We may be fascinated by the elegant style of an historian, but the fascination changes to doubt in the presence of his evident bias and his expressed prejudice.

Mr. Bruce felt his bondage—all slaves felt it—but he has been fair enough, and I may add courageous enough, to say that within his experience and observation, savagery and brutality in the treatment of slaves were the exception and not the rule. The great wrong was in the enslavement *per se* of a fellow-man. Why, he argues, would a man abuse and over-work and starve his slave, a valuable piece of property, any more than he would poorly feed or maltreat his horse or his ox? His own self-interest would require good treatment in order to secure good results from the labor of his slaves. There were harsh, even brutal masters, but Mr. Bruce claims that these were usually found among a class of people who were low bred, and he asserts that the cruelties of slavery could be as easily traced to this class of white men, as we can trace to a similar class to-day the proscriptions, and persecutions and hardships that are suffered by the better element of Colored people.

If left to themselves, Mr. Bruce believes, there would be the best of feeling between the old aristocrat and his former slave, and the world would not be periodically shocked by the intelligence of lynching bees and burnings.

To me, Mr. Bruce's accounts of the old highway system, with the then prevailing modes of travel and trade, are as instructive as they are interesting. But this is only one of the many valuable contributions to history, with which the book abounds.

Mr. Bruce's narration of his experiences begins with his childhood, when he was encouraged by his master to eat and play on his Virginia farm, and carries the reader through the intervening years, until when at Brunswick, practically in charge of his master's business, the war came and changed a nominal freedom into an actual freedom.

Another prominent feature of the book, is Mr. Bruce's contention that the two classes of people in the South should not divide along the line of race or color, and in this connection he furnishes argument to support his condemnation of the common blooded blacks and whites alike, whose bad conduct he asserts has brought shame and disgrace, and misery upon the better classes of white and Colored people of the South.

All the way through the book sets the reader to thinking and whoever may peruse its pages will be amply repaid for his time, and the reader may rest assured that he will not find it a task to read what Mr. Bruce has written. So far from this he will find that, after reading the first page, he will have a desire to read the second page, and his interest will increase to the end of the book

J. H. N. WARING, M. D.,
WASHINGTON, D. C.   Supervisor Public Schools.

————————●————————

WASHINGTON, D. C., *April 19th, 1895.*

I have read in manuscript, Mr. H. C. Bruce's book, "The New Man," and have been greatly interested in its perusal. It gives us a very novel, and I am sure a truthful glimpse of the life of the slave. I think it the only book that fairly represents the relations of the master and slave. Other books have been written on this topic, but they have been written for the purpose of inflaming prejudice, and the horrors of slave life appear to be greatly exaggerated. Mr. Bruce, however, has a simple story to tell and does it well.

This book may be read with profit by the Colored race for the example it affords. The author was a slave until his twenty-ninth year, but by diligence and hard work, in the face of all opposition, he has succeeded in educating himself and gaining positions of honor and trust.

I commend this book to any one who desires to get a true idea of the old-time slave in the cotton fields of the South. THOS. FEATHERSTONHAUGH.

Medical Referee, Bureau of Pensions.

THE NEGRO BOND AND FREE.

We have been permitted to examine the manuscript of a projected book, the subject and the style of which will, we think, prove extremely interesting to the general public. It is the work of a Colored man, a resident of this city, and an employe of the Pension Office—Henry C. Bruce, a brother of Hon. B. K. Bruce, once United States Senator from Mississippi, and latterly Recorder of Deeds from the District of Columbia. It is the unpretentious story, simply and directly told, of a Colored man twenty-nine years a slave. The earlier chapters contain the record of his life during ante-bellum days, his experiences under slavery as a child, youth, and a grown man, the joys, the sorrows, the privations, the pleasures, and the vicissitudes which came to him in turn. The closing chapters tell of the conditions with which emancipation confronted him, what helps and hindrances he encountered in his new career, through what changing fortune he made his way to comfort and independence.

We doubt whether there is to be found in literature anything of its kind at once as authentic and as
entertaining. The writer is not a professional Colored
man. He is not conspicuous in protest against the
attitude of the white people toward the race. He does
not claim to have been a bleeding martyr during his
term of slavery. He does not picture the old southern
proprietor class as monsters and tyrants—quite the
contrary—or pretend that all the virtue, kindness,
worth, and loyalty of that section was to be found in
the Negroes. The fact is, that Mr. Bruce writes of the
period during which he lived in bondage in Virginia,
Mississippi, and Missouri, very much as his own master
would have written—truthfully, fairly, philosophically.
It is evident that he cherishes no resentful feeling
toward those in whose service he spent the first half of
his life. Indeed, one can see that he has for them the
truest affection and regard. If there be one sentiment
which, more than any other, runs through the whole
narrative from beginning to end, it is the sentiment of
pride in the old southern aristocracy, and contempt for
every other type and variety of white man. He is loyal
to his own people, in the highest and truest meaning of
loyalty, but for the slave owners as he knew them, he
has the sense of gratitude and justice strong within
him.

The book is full of wisdom and kindness. Here
and there are touches of shrewd observations which
the Colored people will do well to ponder and reflect
upon. And not the least valuable and creditable feature of Mr. Bruce's work is to be found in the candid,
generous, and fair comment he indulges as to the management of the Pension Office under Messrs. Black,
Raum, and Lochren. It is refreshing, indeed, to find a
Colored man writing so intelligently of slavery during
his own term of bondage, and of race issues and politics,
in which for thirty years past he has been an active, if
a modest and unostentatious participant.—*Washington
Post, April 14, 1895.*

IN THE BLACKS IN THE AMERICAN WEST SERIES

The New Man: Twenty-nine Years a Slave, Twenty-nine Years a Free Man
by H. C. Bruce

Nellie Brown, or The Jealous Wife, with Other Sketches
by Thomas Detter

Shadow and Light: An Autobiography
by Mifflin W. Gibbs

Born to Be
by Taylor Gordon

The Life and Adventures of Nat Love
by Nat Love